ST. ALPHONSUS
125 YEARS
Embracing Our Tradition, Our Faith, Our Future

St. Alphonsus Parish | 125th Anniversary 1888-2014

Copyright © 2014 by St. Alphonsus Parish

All Rights Reserved. This book may not be reproduced, transmitted, or stored in whole or in part by any means, including graphic, electronic, or mechanical without express written consent of the publisher except in the case of brief quotations embodied in critical articles and reviews.

ISBN: 978-1-940164-27-4

Published by:
St. Alphonsus Parish
224 Carrier N.E.
Grand Rapids, Michigan 49505

Professional Photography by: Ruth Parabel Photography
Book layout and design by: Claudia Elzinga and JPL Design Solutions

Printed in the United States of America.

TABLE OF CONTENTS

1	We Are Born	7
2	The Early 1900s	15
3	The 1920s: We're on Fire	21
4	The 1930s: Tough Times	27
5	The 1940s: Big Changes Coming	35
6	The 1950s: The Growing Years	43
7	The 1960s: Cha-cha-changes!	49
8	The 1970s: Turbulent Times	57
9	The Last 25 Years	63
10	The Proud Tradition	71
11	The Redemptorists	81
12	The Fertile Field of Vocations	109
13	Where Your Treasure Is So Lies Your Heart	125
14	The History of Our Organizations	135
15	The Founding Families	141
16	Our Current Organizations	153
17	Our Beautiful Stained Glass Windows	161
18	Congratulation Letters and Papal Proclamation	177
19	Memories	185

FROM THE HEART...

From its founding in 1888, the heart of St. Alphonsus Parish has been beating strongly. We, the writers and readers, are privileged to look back at how the spirit of God inspired and encouraged our brave founders to build and grow this beautiful Parish.

When we read about the beginning of our Parish, it is humbling to imagine the dedication and sacrifice made by our founding families. They worked nights to build our first place to worship God as a community. Men, women and children gathered to work together following their already full day at their jobs. They accomplished this monumental task because they believed. The first Mass of our Parish was held September 2, 1888 in an unfinished orphanage building. Just four months later the dedication of our "first Church" building on January 6, 1889. It would take only four months to build that first Church we would call "home." For 75 years our parish school would function out of that building all because of their commitment and love for our Parish.

And that first Church served this community of worshipers for 20 years until our current Church was built and dedicated in 1909. That building, begun in 1906, would take three years to construct!

Buildings come and go and they are wonderful places to keep the rain and snow off, but the real "heart" of any Parish is the people. Each and every person who has been a part of St. Al's is the author of this book and these stories. This book is about YOU... the stories, the memories, the resilience, perseverance and dedication it takes to make a community. It's about our love for our God and His love for us. If you have been touched, been a part of, been privileged to laugh, to cry, to work hard and sacrifice, and to celebrate... then you already know about this "Heart of St. Alphonsus." It defies definition... It's that place in your heart that recognizes no matter where your journey has taken you—St. Al's is always home and you are always welcome here. Our hearts are full of love and respect for all of the ways God has blessed us over the last 125 years. With this amazing heritage, we look forward for what lies ahead!

We also recognize how we have been incredibly blessed that the Redemptorist Fathers and Dominican Sisters said yes. A courageous yes to be willing to stand shoulder to shoulder, to serve, to teach, and to guide. What an incredible legacy they have written in our hearts.

With great joy this book is dedicated to all of the beautiful hearts that have made this one heart beat strong *"Embracing Our Tradition, Our Faith, Our Future!"*

Andrea Brandt	Karen Eyk	Mary Eyk-Jeakle
Linda Parker	Mary Wysocki	

CHAPTER 1
WE ARE BORN

St. Alphonsus Parish was established in 1888. The Rt. Reverend Bishop Henry Richter received a bequest from lumberman, John Clancy, in the amount of $60,000 following Mr. Clancy's death on April 17, 1884. Mr. Clancy was an immigrant from Ireland who, at the time of his death, was considered among the wealthy men of Grand Rapids in property and finance. Mr. Clancy's intention for the bequest was for an orphan asylum for which plans were begun shortly after his death. Bishop Richter recognized overcrowding of St. Andrew's Cathedral and decided to also use the money to divide the parish, forming a new parish on the north side of Grand Rapids. The parish boundaries would run from East Leonard Street between Reed Street and Coit Avenue, north of Trowbridge Street, east of the Grand River. It included large parts of Grand Rapids, Ada, and Plainfield Township. Land was purchased and a plan was devised to build, not only an orphan asylum, but a church, school, and any other necessary buildings as well. Mr. Clancy's orphanage, St. John's Orphan Asylum, was

The Right Reverend Bishop Henry Richter

Left: John Clancy Monument, St. Andrew's Cemetery, Grand Rapids, MI
Right: John Clancy Obituary, Grand Rapids Daily Eagle

> **OBITUARY – JOHN CLANCY**
>
> In the death of JOHN CLANCY, announced from New York City (which place he had reached on his way home from Europe), a prominent early resident of this city is taken from our community. As he had been in failing health for many years, and as the serious turn of his disease during his visit to the Continent, were he went early last summer, have been well known, the fatal termination was not unexpected, but his many friends here had hoped he might survive at least to reach his home. John Clancy was born in New York City in February 1819. The family came to Michigan in 1835, settling first at Ann Arbor. Ten years later he came to Grand Rapids, and for the next ten years or thereabouts he and his brother WILLIAM (who died about eighteen months ago at Los Angeles, Cal.) were engaged in the grocery trade on Canal street, between Pearl and Lyon. About thirty years ago he sold out of that business and turned his attention to the lumber and real estate trade, in which, in this State and Illinois, he was quite successful, and had accumulated a fair competency in property. In the years from 1858 to 1860 he was a member of the Common Council, and there, by his good judgment and well-directed public spirit, did much to aid in the progress and healthy development of our city. Mr. Clancy was a man of few words, but of decided convictions and strong and genial friendships. In business and financial affairs he was influential and generally successful, one whose counsel was sought and whose opinions carried weight—a respected and useful citizen, with hosts of friends and few or no enemies. In politics he was originally a Democrat, but since the rebellion a Republican. In religious belief he was a conscientious Roman Catholic. As an old resident, and a citizen almost universally known and highly respected in this city and valley, he will be greatly missed, and leaves a pleasant memory. Mr. Clancy never married.
>
> GRAND RAPIDS DAILY EAGLE, Grand Rapids, Mich., Thurs., April 17, 1884, Pg. 2, Col. 1

situated on the block bordered by Lafayette Avenue, Carrier Street, North Avenue, and Leonard Street.

Bishop Richter requested from the Superior General of Rome the assignment of priests for this new parish. This led to the introduction of the Congregation of the Most Holy Redeemer (the Redemptorists) to Grand Rapids. Bishop Richter, upon their arrival from Chicago on August 23, 1888, graciously welcomed Fr. Theodore Lamy, who would become the new pastor and his superior Provincial, the Very Reverend William Lowenkamp. Two days later, Fr. Lamy and Fr. Lowenkamp rented a house at 41 King Ct.—at the corner of King Ct. and Henrietta St. from Maurice Shanahan for $10 per month as their residence. By September 1, 1888 the Redemptorist Community consisting of Fr. Lamy, Pastor, Fr. Terence Clarke, Assistant, and Bro. John Philpot, were settled into the residence.

Getting right to work, on August 26, it was announced at Mass in St. Andrew's Cathedral and St. James' Church that the new parish of St. Alphonsus would begin

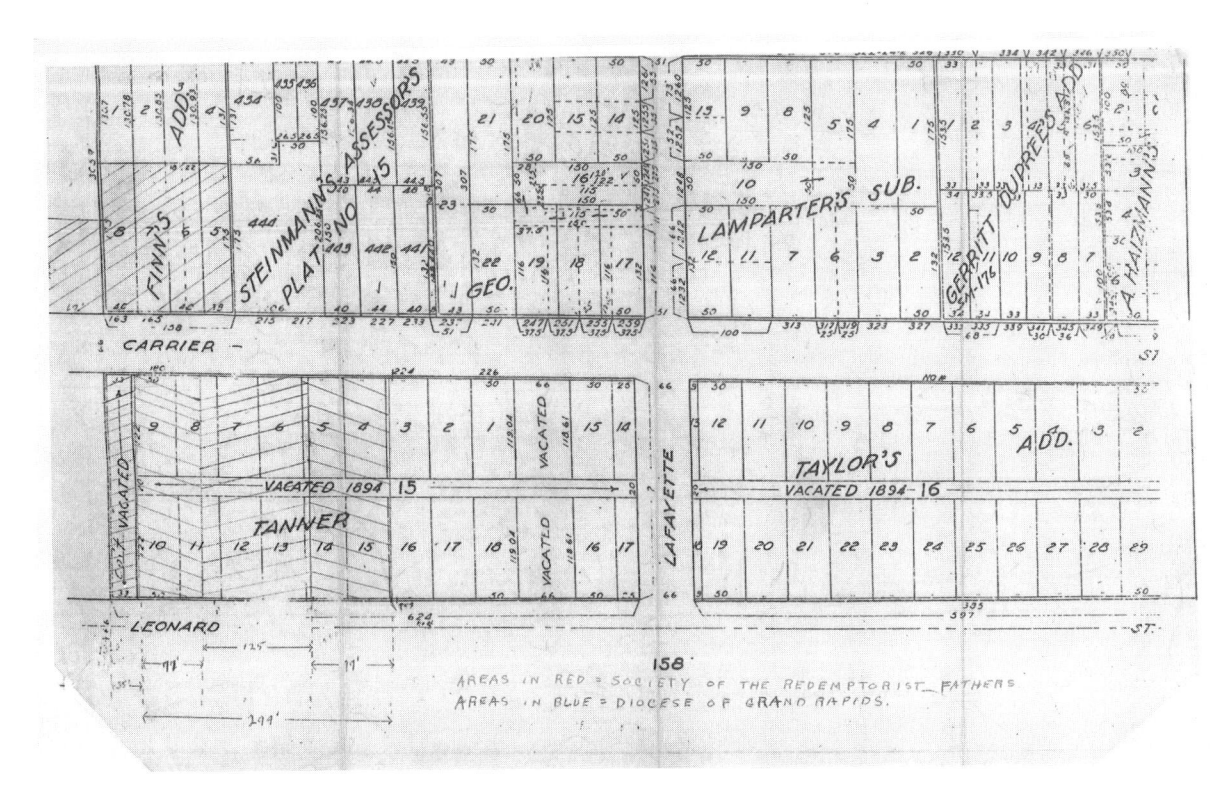

Plot map of the City of Grand Rapids showing the boundaries of the proposed St. Alphonsus Parish

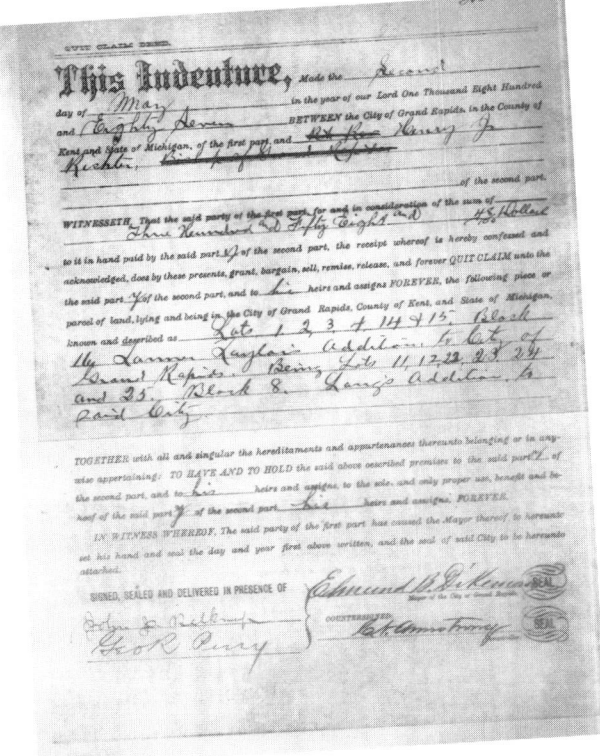

The original land purchase agreement of 1887 for St. John's Orphan Asylum purchased from the City of Grand Rapids by Bishop Richter for $358.48

celebrating Mass on September 2, 1888 at 8:00 A.M. and 10:30 A.M. It was decided that the orphan asylum, as yet unfinished, would be the site for Mass. A room on the first floor was selected as most appropriate and with the permission of the contractors, Haskins and Mander, members of the fledgling parish set about preparing the room. Neighborhood men, women, and children cleaned and furnished the room with 18 backless benches, each 20 feet long. The altar consisted of matching boards across sawhorses, covered with white cotton, and dressed simply with four vases of flowers.

9

SCHOOL DAYS

Original Agreement between Dominican Sisters and the Redemptorists teaching in St. Alphonsus School

The Sisters Agree:

1. To furnish as many competent teachers as shall be necessary to properly conduct the school of St. Alphonsus for both boys and girls.
2. To receive into and teach in each class not less than 45 and not more than 75. Average 60 pupils.
3. To sell to the pupils books and stationery supplied by Father Superior at a price fixed by him and to return receipts for same month to Rev. Father Superior.
4. To furnish a teacher of music when directed by Father Superior.
5. To superintend sweeping and cleaning of school rooms and halls and sweeping of closets.
6. To direct and superintend the annual examinations and exhibitions.
7. To collect and receipt the tuition pay of pupils (if any is to be collected) monthly and hand same with statement to Rev. Father Superior.
8. To open no school or academy within the limits of St. Alphonsus Parish without the consent of the V.Rev. Fr. Provincial C.Ss.R. of St. Louis, MO.

The Father Superior Agrees:

1. To pay for each and every such teacher the sum of $20.00 per month for ten months in each and every year during the term of this contract.
2. To furnish all school furniture, books, and stationery and heating of school rooms.
3. To furnish (but only one) for each teacher: bed, bedding, table, chair and wash stand.
4. To give one quarter of net proceeds of exhibition conducted by sisters for benefit of school to the sisters. It is understood that no exhibition or entertainment is to be given without the consent and approval of the Rev. Fr. Superior. To rescind this contract 3 months notice in writing much be given.

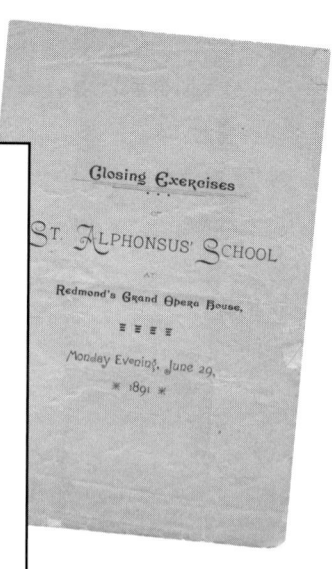

1891 St. Alphonsus graduation program

The original teaching agreement between the Dominican Sisters and the Redemptorists for St. Alphonsus School

1896 St. Alphonsus graduation program

Dominican Sisters & Mothers Superior

10

St. John's Orphan Asylum Grand Rapids, MI

Fr. Lamy and Fr. Clarke provided the vestments, chalice, and other requisites for the celebration of Mass, having brought them from Chicago. The Provincial, Fr. Lowenkamp preached a sermon on "Build a House for God and He Will Build a House for You" at both Masses, which were well attended. Following the 10:30 A.M. Mass, St. Alphonsus Parish celebrated its first baptism. The newly baptized child was Bernard Roche.

The following Sunday, September 9, the Masses were again celebrated at the as yet unenclosed orphan asylum. Cotton sheeting was tacked to the walls at the windows due to inclement weather. The gusty windows blew down the protective sheeting, blowing out the candles as well. John Broffee and William Kelly, two young men of the parish, followed the example of two small boys from the 8:00 A.M. Mass and proudly, diligently, and protectively held the candles keeping them lit throughout the Mass. Later that same day, arrangements were made to have future services held at Finn's Hall, 39 Plainfield Road, just south of Leonard Street. on the west side of the road, next to the Baldwin House Hotel, until better accommodations could be provided. Patrick Finn agreed to the use of his hall on Saturdays, Sundays, and holy days free of charge for six months. He included in this promise the use of the wood stove and

Finn's Hall was located at 39 Plainfield. In 1888 it served as a temporary meeting place for the St. Alphonsus congregation. *St. Alphonsus Catholic Church Grand Rapids, MI 1914. Grand Rapids Public Library, 347-17.5)*.

Finn's Hall, located at 39 Plainfield Avenue, Grand Rapids (courtesy of the Grand Rapids Public Library)

necessary wood. Masses were held at Finn's Hall beginning September 16. Two daily Masses were celebrated in the parlor at the pastoral residence at 41 King Court. The week of September 9 saw the completion of the plans for the new

11

St. Alphonsus combination church and school.

Ground was broken for the new building on Saturday, September 15, 1888. The cornerstone of the new St. Alphonsus Parish Church/School was laid on October 14, 1888. Remarks for the day mention the favorable weather, thousands of rejoicing Catholics, and eager spectators for the celebration. The imposing ceremonies began with a parade including the current City Council President and Chief Marshal Alderman Maurice Shanahan and his aides, police platoons, various associations and societies from the city's Catholic churches, and a 10-piece Polish band beginning at the intersection of E. Bridge and Canal Street (now Michigan Street and Monroe Avenue). The groups proceeded to the Redemptorist's residence on King Court where Bishop Richter, priests from St. Alphonsus, St. Andrew's Cathedral, St. James', St. Mary's, St. Adalbert's parishes, and Redemptorists from Chippewa Falls, Wisconsin and Detroit, Michigan, joined them. The procession moved through Page, Perry, and Quimby Streets to Plainfield Avenue, then up East Leonard Street to the site of the new building where they were met by a group of people estimated to be between five and eight thousand. Bishop Richter preached a brief, impressive sermon following the laying of the cornerstone. Fr. Goldsmith from Wisconsin gave a brief history of Catholicity in Grand Rapids. Shanahan came forward to test that the cornerstone was properly laid. He followed this with appropriate remarks for laying a solid foundation for the parish. Everyone in attendance was given the opportunity to test the cornerstone and determine whether it was properly laid to serve as a proper foundation for the parish.

The original Church and School circa 1880s

There was a hearty response from the audience in the collection of nearly $700 in cash and a number of subscriptions as well. The building of the St. Alphonsus Parish Church/School proceeded rapidly. The dedication of the new building would be held by January 1889.

The Holy Name Society, the first organized in the Grand Rapids Diocese, was organized on February 12, 1899. The group consisted of 25 men from the newly established parish.

Cornerstone of St. Alphonsus, 1888

LAETITIA TRAVERSE, FIRST GRADUATE OF ST. ALPHONSUS SCHOOL.

Maurice Shanahan, an outstanding benefactor and staunch financial supporter of St. Alphonsus, in its early days, conferred on her the gold medal for general excellence.

CHAPTER 2
THE EARLY 1900S

The parish was quickly growing out of the combination church and school building by 1901. Some accounts said that by 1901 the number of families had grown to 260. Collections began to fund the building of this new worship space. Not unlike many fundraisers to come, there were lots of suppers and entertainments held by the various groups and societies.

Fr. George Hild, pastor, wrote in the annals for the parish on March 10, 1905: "… the Provincial Very Rev. Jos. Firle, C.Ss.R with two of his consulters arrived to locate the site for the new Church. It was agreed to call a mass meeting of the men of the parish on St. Patrick's night after the services. Approximately 100 men were present. Because of diversity of opinion no fitting location could be decided on."

One of the members and large donors interested in building our new church was Maurice Shanahan. He was the treasurer of the Bissell Carpet Sweeping Company. Shanahan's imposing hilltop residence, which was completed in 1882, had a clear view to the future site of our new church. Mike Page reports in the Creston Neighborhood Association newsletter, The North End Connection in 2014, that "The original plans for St. Alphonsus Church had the front of the church on Leonard St. It was common for a major structure to front on a main street. However, the story goes that Maurice Shanahan, well known politician, respected business man, and major donor for the church's construction, said he wanted the church to face north in the direction of his house on the hill at Plainfield

View of St. Alphonsus from the Shanahan home

Road and Grove Street. That way, he would see the beautiful front of the church when he looked out the windows of his home." (Maurice Shanahan was buried from the church one year after its completion and dedication in 1909.)

The contracts awarded on March 17, 1906 were as follows: brick work was awarded to the Bonhagke Bros. of Ionia for $16,456. The carpenter work was awarded to Julius Koeln of Grand Rapids for $11,850. Bishop Richter laid the cornerstone on May 6, 1906, as reported in The Grand Rapids Press. He stated that this would be the first church building that had been erected in Grand Rapids since the diocese was formed.

However, the progress of the "newest" church was slow and problem ridden. From problems with the footings to threats of lawsuits with different contractors, the church

Cornerstone of St. Alphonsus, 1906

A MOVER & SHAKER

Mr. Maurice Shanahan was a driving force in the establishment of St. Alphonsus Church. His home, located on Grove Street near Plainfield, overlooked the permanent location of the new church. Upon his death in 1909, Mr. Shanahan was buried in Mt. Calvary Cemetery in Grand Rapids, MI.

Portrait of Maurice Shanahan

City of Grand Rapids street sign

Shanahan monument, Mt. Calvary Cemetery, Grand Rapids, MI

The Shanahan House

Early view of the landscape around the new Church

took a long time to be completed. From the "Silver Jubilee Booklet" it tells us that when the new pastor, Rev. Joseph Chapoton, arrived on the scene and saw the church standing unfinished (while the old hall was far too small for the large congregation) he became determined to complete the new church. With his characteristic energy, he threw himself heart and soul into the work. By his earnestness and zeal, he easily gained the good will of the entire parish. After six or seven weeks of hard,

St. Alphonsus Church Bell

Inscription on St. Alphonsus Church Bell

untiring effort—fathers and people working hand in hand—the church was completed. A lot of the men in the parish would come to work in the church after working all day in the furniture factories. Most of them put in 10 to 12 hours a day on their regular jobs and then they would work until dark helping the carpenters and bricklayers. Pride and determination brought the project to completion.

St. Alphonsus Graduating Class of 1904

On December 22, 1909 history reads: "Today was a memorable day for the people of this parish on account of the consecration of the new church. The services began at 6 o'clock in the morning, and were conducted by the Rt. Rev. Bishop Richter of the diocese, Fr. Breffeil, C.Ss.R. was the deacon and Fr. M. Meyer, C.Ss.R., was subdeacon."

Ladies of the Parish

Once the church was finished, plans began to remodel the school as it too had grown too small to accommodate the 300 students that were now enrolled. By 1912, Fr. Chapoton was transferred and Fr. E.K. Cantwell came as the new pastor. Fr. Cantwell decided that remodeling the school was not enough as enrollment continued to grow. He decided to build a new school and a new pastoral residence. Again, in the spirit of the wonderful community there were card parties, suppers, and entertainments by the societies. The people of the parish worked nobly to raise the required funds. In June of 1913, the fathers' house was moved and remodeled and on August 26, 1913 ground was broken for the new school. On February 15, 1914, the dedication of the Silver Jubilee (which had been put off from the fall of 1913) and the new school building were combined with nearly all of the former pastors and priests in attendance. Nearly all of the Catholic clergy and laity of the city joined in to celebrate this wonderful moment in the history of St. Alphonsus.

View of the inside of the early Church

CHAPTER 3
THE 1920S: WE'RE ON FIRE!

There were two roof fires in the school. Around dinnertime, the St. Alphonsus School janitor reported the first, on January 17, 1921. The City Fire Department used the water hose to extinguish the roof fire. Despite this, there was no interruption of classes the next morning, or the card party the next evening hosted by the Married Ladies of the Holy Family. The janitor reported the probable cause of the fire was inferior coal and a shingle roof.

The second fire, on March 21, 1928, demonstrated the advantage of the random fire drills carried out by the Dominican Sisters' staff throughout the years. A passerby pulled the box on the corner and alerted the sisters to the fire. The firemen from Engine House No. 5 responded to fight the blaze shortly before noon. By the time they arrived, the sisters had quietly guided the school children from first to eighth grades onto the grounds and away from danger. The Grand Rapids Press reported the next day that fire officials were unstinting in their praise of the sisters and the students, who displayed not a sign of disorder. The probable cause of this fire was sparks from the chimney landing on the wooden shingles.

Redemptorist Rectory

How many of us remember the fire drill alarm sounding and Sister say-

21

Original convent of the Dominican Sisters, Grand Rapids, MI

ing, "Quickly, children! Single file, with your finger over your lips!" How quickly we could file out of the building with Sr. Ursuline or Sr. Emma standing nearby with her stopwatch.

1928 St. Alphonsus Boys Track Team

November 23, 1926, saw the beginning of Beano games held by the Holy Name Society as a means of raising funds for the treasury. The prizes were five pounds of sugar or canned goods. That was also when the Country Store was begun. The country farmers would donate chickens or vegetables and they were placed in a basket, chances were sold—three for a quarter—and they'd spin the wheel and see who won.

On June 24, 1928 a beautiful statue of St. Therese, The Little Flower, and shrine were blessed and dedicated by pastor, Rev. C.J. Harrison, C.Ss.R. Someone who had received a favor while in ill health donated the statue in gratitude. Another improvement during 1928 was in the appearance of the school with a new roof, window painting, a new playground, and parking spaces for automobiles.

Memories from students include attending 8:00 A.M. daily Mass.

WHERE WE PRAY

While prayer can occur in many places and in a variety of situations, our church provides a wonderful location for reflection. The vastness of the church was complimented by side altars that provided intimate spots for personal prayer. Through these special sites, devotion to Our Mother of Perpetual Help and St. Gerard were fostered in the hearts of St. Alphonsus parishioners.

Inside the Church 1914 (before stained glass windows)

Our Mother of Perpetual Help side altar

Left: St. Gerard side altar
Right: The high altar of St. Alphonsus Church

Then, while taking attendance, Sister would ask what time you arrived at mass, grade you from 0 to 5 depending on your arrival for Mass, and send a monthly note home to your parents. One person remembers sneaking up on the church roof bell tower and throwing snowballs at the people coming to Mass. The way he remembers it, the kids would throw a couple snowballs and duck down behind the tower wall. As he recalls, most people never figured out where the snowballs came from.

The Holy Name Society also presented its first Minstrel Show, entitled "Making Whoopee," in February 1929. There were seven special presentations in addition to the Whoopee Minstrels and several longstanding St. Alphonsus families were represented: the Deschaine's, the Veneklase's, the Thiel's, the Hanrahan's, and the Conlon's. The net profit for the minstrel show was approximately $200.

Other memories from parishioners include the school band—com-

School Band circa 1920s

posed of 20 to 30 students—sitting between the stairwells in the halls and playing as the students marched into school. The band played very spirited music! Another person remembers the honor of taking the sisters, who taught school and lived at St. John's Home, their breakfast. They brought the food, slid it in through the window, and then brought the dirty dishes back. The best part was missing school while you did this task! One of the more exciting events that occurred during the 1920s was a visit to St. John's Home by Babe Ruth. Ruth was raised in an orphanage and made a point of visiting one in each new city he visited. The Yankees had an exhibition game at Ramona Park that year and the parishioner remembers running up to the orphanage with his friends after school.

Young members of the congregation

View from St. John's Home of the campus as it existed in the 1930s

CHAPTER 4
THE 1930S: TOUGH TIMES

The Married Ladies' Sodality hosted a card party to raise money to supplement donations for new carpeting in the church sanctuary in April 1931. Additional funds were raised by private donations and other entertainment events for children. The carpet was purchased for $1,092 from Wurzburg's Department Store.

The Liguori Players presented a farce, "The Whole Town's Talking," in April 1935 in the St. Alphonsus School Auditorium. Long-time St. Alphonsus families were represented in the cast... Ruth Hummel, Margaret Mary Nulty, Bob Heitz, Roger Shields, Lorraine McCormick, Eugene Schmidt, Maxine Foley, Grace Bek, Luella Kosminski, and Dan Foley. The funds raised by the Liguori Players productions were used for St. Alphonsus Parish charitable purposes.

First Communion Class, 1938

The Girl's Service Squad was organized in September 1937. The group consisted of 25 girls who assisted the first and second graders in dressing and cleaning chalkboards and erasers daily.

The first parish Fall Festival was held in the parking lot in 1938. A memory from that day holds, "It poured rain the first day. They had a big circus tent, but we were still sloshing around in water up to our ankles. I think that was the only year it was held outside. The rain cured that."

The Holy Name Society began their parish breakfasts in the 1930s.

In September 1938, some of the seventh and eighth grade girls began wearing uniforms. The plan was to expand the uniforms to girls from fifth to eighth grades the following year.

Two memories from students in 1938 include the election of the new pope, Pope Pius XII, on March 2. "Over our radio we could hear the crowds cheering, and then the Pope gave his blessing in a clear, inspiring voice." Another student remembered in the March 13, 1938 School Annals; "We had the afternoon free in honor of the Coronation of the Holy Father on the day previous."

The West Michigan Catholic, on November 6, 1938, reported the celebration of the St. Alphonsus Parish 50 Year Jubilee. They also recognized the Redemptorist Fathers as the founders. The religious ceremonies were attended by "the most notable gatherings of Catholic clergy assembled here in years." The Jubilee Banquet provided an opportunity for church and civic leaders to honor the parish and its spiritual leaders. Congratulations were sent from religious throughout the country.

First Communion Class, 1938

TIDBITS FROM SOME "ALMOST" FOUNDING FAMILIES

It takes many dedicated hearts to build a strong parish! The early families at St. Alphonsus helped the newly-formed parish continue to grow in the next decades. Over 100 years later, descendants of these early families still play an important part in our church.

The Page Family

They can trace their roots back to 1902 when William and Margaret Page—along with their three young children—joined the newly formed St. Al's. Their family quickly grew to include six children who all attended the grade school, the three youngest being baptized there and all receiving further sacraments from our parish. William Page was a master wood carver and would share that talent with the growing church. He carved the original wood frames for the Stations of the Cross which remained on the church walls until the extensive renovation in 1987. In 1934, William retired from his career and took a part-time job as the janitor for the school and church.

Charlies & Lucille Page, Dorthy & Harry Mika, Lucy O'Rourke

The youngest of the six children was Charles "Charlie" Page who was born in 1912. He received all of his sacraments at St. Al's as well as attending and graduating from the school in 1928. Fast forward and Charlie meets a gal from St. Al's, Lucille

TIDBITS, CONT.

(Veneklase), who becomes his beautiful bride in May of 1941. They went on to have eight children who also all attended St. Alphonsus School. Charlie and Lucille were very active members of the parish and you will read about their involvement in different places of this book. One of their other "claims to fame" is that one of their offspring became a diocesan priest and holds the title in the Redemptorist community as 'the one that got away" from the Page Street legacy!

The Bek/Fortier Family

John and Mabel Bek were the second couple to get married in the newly constructed St. Alphonsus Church on June 30, 1910. From that day on, a great love for this parish developed in this family and all of their descendants. They purchased and donated the statue of St. Alphonsus, which sits above the doors outside of the church. When the time came that the baldachin arrived from Italy, John stored it in his garage while workers removed part of the wall to get it moved into the church. Due to the weight of the baldachin, some of the floor was also taken up and later re-laid to anchor the baldachin directly into the foundation.

John and Mabel Bek Family, 1944
Bob, Marion, Grace, Ruth, Jack

TIDBITS, CONT.

The Bek's had five children: Robert Louise who married Edith Emery, Marion Rosalie who married Thomas Roach, Grace Barbara who married Leo Fortier, Ruth Margaret who married William Manning and John Joseph who married Mary Jane Reynolds.

The Fortier's Leo & Grace, Barbara, Leo, Danny, Patty, Mike, & Virginia, 1953

John and Marie (often called Mabel) had many residences in the neighborhood including 165 Carrier which was the old Finn family home. They later built a house at 333 Carrier which, after their death, was purchased by Grace (daughter) and Leo Fortier and their family. When Grace passed away her grandson, Ken Fortier, purchased the house in 2013. 101 years later, the house that John Bek built is still in the family.

Mabel Tooher c 1903, John Bek c 1900

One other of many interesting co-incidences is that Mary (Mabel)'s father, William Tooher, was baptized at St. Andrew's Cathedral on May 30, 1866. His godfather was Patrick Finn. This is the same Patrick Finn, who in 1888, when St. Alphonsus was formed, volunteered his hall for Mass from September of 1888 through January of 1889!

St. Alphonsus Graduating Class, 1939

The altar was amassed with golden yellow chrysanthemums. The church was filled to capacity. The Most Rev. Gerald C. Murray, C.Ss.R., D.D., Bishop of Saskatoon, Saskatchewan, Canada, a Redemptorist himself before being appointed as bishop, sang a Pontifical High Mass and preached the sermon. Pope Pius XII granted permission to Bishop Murray to officiate the Jubilee Mass and sent his felicitations and congratulatory message through the Apostolic Delegate to the United States. Archbishop Edward A. Mooney of Detroit and Governor Frank Murphy were also in attendance.

The Redemptorist Rector Major in Rome requested the Papal Benediction. Bishop Murray imparted it as delegated by Bishop Joseph G. Pinten. The Pope's communication to the congregation was read in Latin and English by Rev. Robert W. Bogg, St. Stephen's Parish pastor and vice chancellor of the diocese.

The Sunday afternoon Jubilee Banquet was held following the morning Mass. Rev. John A. Gabriels of Resurrection Church, Lansing, acted as toastmaster. "Our Holy Father" was the topic of Bishop Murray's speech. Rt. Rev. Msgr.

Daniel Ryan, LL.D., president of Sacred Heart Seminary, Detroit, presented "Our Archdiocese." Most Rev. William O'Brien, D.D., L.D. was represented by Rev. Richard St. John spoke on "The Missions." More than 300 members and friends of the parish attended the Mass and Jubilee Banquet.

St. Alphonsus Boys Basketball Team, 1933

Early School Band, 1930s

CHAPTER 5
THE 1940S: BIG CHANGES COMIN'

The Finn family again made another generous contribution to the parish. The Finn's house was once located in the St. Alphonsus' convent parking lot. The parish moved the house over to Leonard Street. St. Alphonsus Parish then held a raffle for the home.

The Sisters were able to have their first Midnight Mass in their convent chapel in 1941. It was described as follows, in <u>The St. Alphonsus Convent Journal</u>, on December 24, 1941:

"Santa came at five o'clock. What a lovely time! We were all like children when it came to opening our packages and letters. We could not enjoy them very long as we went to Midnight Mass and as we had the two following Masses in our own little chapel. We had to clear away our things and make ready for this blessed event—our first Midnight Mass in our own little chapel.

Breakfast was served immediately after at which all our Sisters were pres-

Dominican nuns with Christmas tree

35

ent. Father Cantwell had breakfast with us and we certainly enjoyed it.

As the Sisters that stay up at the Home (St. John's Orphanage) had to sing a High Mass at 5:30 A.M. we sat up and helped keep them awake. We retired at 5:30 A.M. after the Sisters had left and got a little "Shut Eye" until later.

First outdoor crib in the City of Grand Rapids 1940

Some of the Sisters attended other Masses over at the Church. I forgot to tell how beautiful our Midnight Mass at the Church was.

The beautiful crib outdoors was lighted and Christmas Carols were sung by the choir.

At the appointed time girls dressed as angels floated into the sanctuary and up the aisle of the Church singing carols. The Mass began and the singing was most beautiful. It was the first Midnight Mass in 15 years. One would think when the time came for Communion that all the people in Grand Rapids were receiving at that Mass. It was both beautiful and edifying."

Tearing down the old Dominican convent, October 1948

Another entry into the convent journal speaks of how excited the Sisters were at the prospect of getting their own confessional. January 9, 1942:

"Fr. Powers of St. Andrew's has been appointed Confessor for the remainder of the year. Fr. Heinge is making a confessional: we are anxious to see it.

The confessional has been sent over. It is so big, that we cannot get it in the house. We told Sister Madeline Sophie we had to go to Confession out on the side porch. In her serious way she said, "I will

MAJESTY OF ITALIAN MARBLE IN THE NEW ALTAR
Excerpts from the story of the Baldachin

The new central altar of St. Alphonsus Catholic Church is made of marble imported from the Pietrasanta and the Carrara district of Italy. The project included two side altars and a pulpit, also of Italian marble, which has been delayed by lack of electric power for quarrying since the Nazis destroyed the 1,000 year old aqueducts which formerly brought water from the mountains and are used in modern times to generate electricity. An altar and communion railing for the parish convent also awaits arrival of a fourth shipment of marble from Italy, Fr. Daly said. The 75-ton altar and baldachin stand on a 38-ton foundation of reinforced concrete. Four marble columns 25 feet high support the baldachin, which is surmounted by Gothic spires, the highest of which is 50 feet above the floor. The Harold R. Sobie Company did the structural work; Wilfred P. McLaughlin was the architect. J.L. Hogan Construction Company built the foundation and Custom Interiors did the background. All companies are from Grand Rapids.

never go out there." Sister called Fr. Cantwell and told him of our distress. He said, "Tell Sister Francis de Sales or Sister Hedwig to make one." Sister Francis de Sales took a window screen and an old bed screen and made one. Sister John Marie painted it."

When I read the Sisters accounts it makes me laugh and think of Ingrid Bergman in the classic film, "The Bells of St. Mary's."

Holy Name Society Variety Show, 1949

PLANS FOR THE NEW CONVENT

The Sisters finally got their new two-story brick and steel convent in 1949. It was located at 205 Carrier NE, now the site of the Carrier Crest Apartments.

Bishop Haas, in a report in the parish bulletin on May 12, 1946, authorized a drive be started on January 1, 1947 for a new convent for the Dominican Sisters. One parishioner remembered that a Bond Drive was started after World War II. People were asked to turn in their war bonds to help finance the new convent. The Holy Name Society's minutes detail that in March 1947, Fr. John Daly, pastor, announced his plans for the new convent at their meeting. Captains and solicitors were chosen and a Kick-Off Dinner was given for the Convent Fund campaign workers. The Holy Name Minstrel Show, which was discontinued during the war years, was also resumed. The show was held in April of 1948, with the funds raised going to furnishing the chapel of the soon to be built convent.

REBUILDING AFTER A SECOND FIRE

St. Alphonsus School had another fire on March 21, 1945. This fire began in the basement and destroyed part of the school building and parish society meeting places. The parish then leased Shanahan Hall on Plainfield Avenue for all parish activities. The necessary repairs, restoration, and renovation to the school as well as the modernization of the lavatories were also authorized in the bulletin of May 12, 1946. A two-classroom prefabricated all-steel building was erected to handle the increase in enrollment.

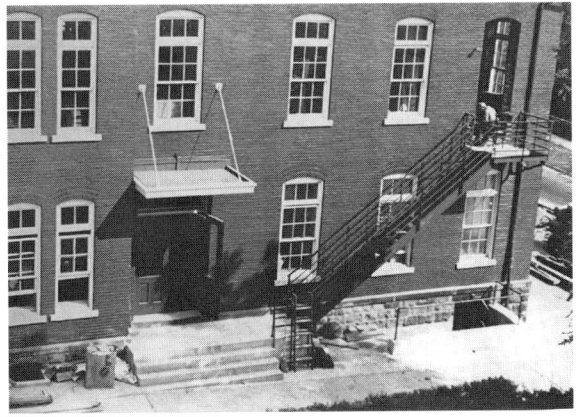

St. Alphonsus School fire escape, September 10 1946

Invitations were issued by pastor, the Very Rev. John F. Daly, C.Ss.R., for Christmas Midnight Mass in gratitude for the people's cooperation with the St. Alphonsus Parish Plan and use of weekly Sunday envelopes. The invitation for a reserved pew was to be presented to an usher at the door.

CHANGES COMING TO ST. AL'S

The feeling of family was tested in 1946 when the parish was divided. New boundaries were set and Blessed Sacrament Parish was formed. Families living north of Knapp Street, approximately 400 St. Alphonsus families, became part of Blessed Sacrament Parish. Then, Blessed Sacrament Parish was split and St. Jude Parish was established. A parishioner recalled, "Some of our families sold their houses and moved back inside St. Al's boundaries. They wanted their kids to go to school here, get married here, and live in this parish. Just like them and their parents. We're a family parish."

The new convent

World War II affected the St. Alphonsus family as it did all the nation's families. Sr. Augustina was put in charge of the bailer purchased by the school. Children and families saved paper, rags, iron, and rubber to support the war effort. Masses were again held in the school because the coal shortage did not allow for heating the church. Special prayers were said for our service men through the Mother of Perpetual Help, Adopt-a-Yank Club program. The Novena services were always crowded. The Holy Name Society held its annual Mother's Day Breakfast in May 1944. A collection was taken

Moving the house for the new Dominican convent, October 1948

and a new plaque was purchased with names of all the Boys in Service. The plaque was placed in Church at the Shrine of Our Lady of Perpetual Help.

The Holy Name Society celebrated its Golden Jubilee on February 13, 1949. The 50th anniversary celebration was detailed in *The Western Michigan Catholic Weekly*, on September 19, 1957, in an issue describing the St. Alphonsus Parish's 70th year:

Holy Name Golden Jubilee Banquet at the Pantlind Hotel 1949

"The celebration began with a Solemn High Mass in the presence of the late Bishop Francis J. Haas. Father James A. Ostrander, C.Ss.R., spiritual director of the society was the celebrant and Father John J. Britz, C.Ss.R., present pastor, and Father Raymond Schmitt, C.Ss.R., pastor of Holy Name parish, Omaha, Nebr., were Deacon and Subdeacon, respectively.

Both Frs. Schmitt and Britz had been former spiritual directors of the society.

Father T. Vincent McKenna, now pastor of St. Margaret's, Otsego, acted as Master of Ceremonies.

Father Francis Schultz, C.Ss.R., member of the faculty of Catholic University of America, Washington, D.C preached the sermon.

Following the Mass the Bishop blessed the cornerstone of the new Sisters' convent. Father John F. Daly, C.Ss.R., then pastor of St. Alphonsus assisted him.

Holy Name Society Procession 1949

A dinner was held at the Pantlind at noon with Bishop Haas and Atty. Joseph Schnitzler, Mount Pleasant, as speakers. Ernest T. Conlin, who had been president of the society from 1922 to 1924, acted as toastmaster.

Louis Hillary then was president of the Holy Name. The president today is Thomas Michmerhuizen."

THE STORY OF THE BALDACHIN

The baldachin at St. Alphonsus was also a product of WWII. It was a project of pastor, the Very Rev. John F. Daly. The lay people of the parish approached the Most Rev. Francis J. Haas, D.D., Bishop of Grand Rapids telling him, "They're starving in Italy. We need to build the Baldachin. They've got to have some work over there."

Scaffolding in the Church to support the new work, January 28, 1947

St. Alphonsus Baldachin (1981 photo)

Bishop Haas approved the installation of a new marble high altar, two marble side altars in the sanctuary, and a marble pulpit. He also authorized cleaning and redecorating of the interior of the Church, repainting of all exterior buildings, repairing of all sidewalks, rebuilding of the Leonard Street wall, and asphalting of the parking lots and playgrounds.

The high altar with baldachin were completed and described in an article in *The Grand Rapids Herald* on Wednesday, December 28, 1949.

CHAPTER 6
THE 1950S: THE GROWING YEARS

Things were starting to change. In the early 1950s, the Young Ladies' Sodality group dissolved, due to very little activity. The many married and expectant women of the parish formed the St. Gerard's Guild. The group would meet in someone's home and sew and talk. They made baby clothes for the expectant mothers. When you had a baby you received a layette no matter your social and financial status. There was a place for everyone. The older ladies often knitted sweaters and booties and made the finer and nicer items. The members who didn't sew well made diapers.

Classroom, February 17, 1954

St. Alphonsus School was the only school in Grand Rapids with two softball teams in April 1955. So many boys arrived for the first practice that they were compelled to form two teams. There was a team for the 7th grade boys, coached by Edward Wolford. Alex Laggis coached the 8th grade team.

Sadly, the Fall Festival, which supported many projects in the parish, was received with a lack of enthusiasm in October of 1955. The decision was made in March 1956 to forego future festivals. Parishioners

IS THIS SEAT TAKEN?

The pew rental was still in effect.

One of the ushers remembers, *"When I first started ushering, in the fifties, we collected pew rent on the first collection. It used to be a dime, but then it went up to a quarter. We carried a ton of nickels, dimes, and quarters in a wooden tray, so we could make change. I used to think that someday Christ was going to come into the church with a knotted cord and drive the money changers from the temple again."*

Pews in St. Alphonsus Church

Ladies of the Holy Family Program, May 4, 1958

were given Fall Festival Substitute Funds envelopes instead.

The St. Alphonsus CARA Club was formed in June 1956 by a group of men in the parish. Their mission was to stimulate, promote, and help the young people of St. Alphonsus develop and take part in various athletic, recreational, and allied programs. All of the programs were available to both boys and girls. Eligibility did not require affiliation with any special youth group already established in the parish. Charles Page was the first President of the CARA Club. They have remained very active throughout the years.

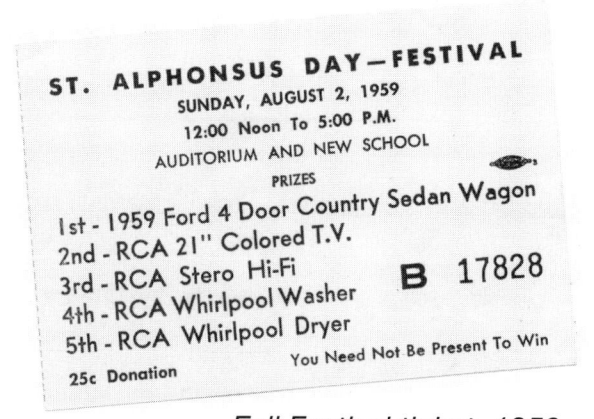

Fall Festival ticket, 1959

Catholic Daughter's Mass

The bills were coming in for the growth of the parish. The St. Alphonsus bulletin, in October 1956, presented the facts. The Sisters' convent had a debt of $60,000. The approximate cost of the new school was $224,000. Interest on the loans due in 1957 was $12,000. There were 183 students from St. Alphonsus attending Catholic Central High School with an amount of $24 per student assessed to the parish. The exciting news was that we had 636 stu-

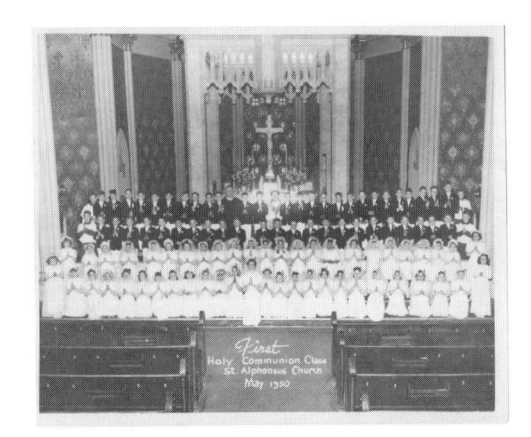

First Communion, May 1950

The envelope collection in June 1957 reflected an average of 5 categories: 325 contributors of $3 or more, 181 contributors of $2 to $3, 337 contributors of $1 to $2, 246 contributors of $1, and 167 families not returning their Sunday envelopes.

dents attending the grade school with a projected number of 800 students in 1957.

The parishioners were asked to increase their weekly tithe to meet the growing bills. Families were encouraged to donate $3 weekly.

Fundraising dinner, 1950s

May breakfast in the new school

The new organ was dedicated in May 1957 with a chorus of 50 people directed by Joseph L. Sullivan and Joan Boucher and members of the Grand Rapids String Quartet performing a Church Sonata by Mozart. Mrs. Louise (Imperi) Labozzetta, soprano, was the soloist, accompanied by the new organ, harp, and violin. The organ had 895 pipes with arrangements for an additional 332. The cost of each organ pipe was $10. Parishioners were asked to offset the cost of the new organ by contributing to the Organ Fund over five months.

Picture of the Pipe Organ

times, Fr. Britz contributed as a missionary, first assistant at Holy Redeemer Parish in Detroit, and commissioned as a Chaplain in the U.S. Army. In September 1957 Fr. Britz was the head of community at St. Alphonsus consisting of nine priests and one lay brother. Fr. Edwin Smith and Fr. Francis J. Fagen served as his first and second assistants respectively.

May Crowning 1958

Fr. John J. Britz, C.Ss.R. returned in 1955 to serve his second term as St. Alphonsus pastor. He previously served in that capacity from 1924 to 1927. Between these

St. Alphonsus School Bus

CHAPTER 7
THE 1960S: CHA-CHA-CHA-CHANGES!

Fr. Seifert celebrated the 50th anniversary of his ordination into the priesthood on September 5, 1961. Janie (Bardwell) Olejniczak remembered Fr. Seifert by his poem that so many of us think of each spring. "Spring has sprung. The grass is riz. I wonder where dem flowers is."

In the 1960s, our parish priests were such a presence in the community. They would frequently walk in our neighborhood on Lafayette and Coldbrook Streets. Fr. Seifert, Fr. Fagen, Fr. O'Connor, and Fr. Langton were always stopping by to visit. Meanwhile, Fr. Oelerich was usually at the men's city softball games at Mary Waters Park remembers Mary (Eyk) Jeakle.

A last look (sister with cross and first cornerstone)

Sunday, September 29, 1963 marked the Diamond Jubilee celebration for St. Alphonsus Parish with a Mass attended by the Most Rev. Allen J. Babcock, Bishop of Grand Rapids, and offered by the Very Rev. John N. McCormick, Provincial Superior of the Redemptorist Fathers. Fr. John J. Britz, C.Ss.R., former pastor, preached the sermon.

Fr. Edmund Langton, Pastor, reading to a parish family c. 1960

A Requiem Mass was held on Saturday for the Parish with a memorial sermon given by former pastor, Fr. John Daly, C.Ss.R. A children's Mass was also held on Monday, celebrated by Fr. Raymond Schmitt, C.Ss.R., former parish priest and now assistant to the provincial.

A three-month, $31,000 refurbishing of the interior of the church was completed for the Jubilee. Existing murals were restored. Walls and ceilings were treated with variations of rose stone, turquoise, chinchilla, and gold leaf. The revised lighting enhanced the color scheme.

Most Rev. Charles A. Salatka, Auxiliary Bishop left for Rome to attend Vatican Council II, Ecumenical Conclave. Most Rev. Allen J. Babcock would leave in October. The Council, begun by Pope John XXIII, is now directed by Pope Paul VI to address six major areas:

1. Allow parts of the Mass to be said in English or appropriate modern language.
2. Decentralize the administration of the Church.
3. Encourage Catholics to study the bible.
4. Give a more important role in Catholic life to the laity.

Diamond Jubilee Celebration, September 1963

5. Place the Church unequivocally on record in favor of religious freedom for all.
6. Modify canon laws on mixed marriages.

Forty Hours Devotion of the Jubilee was held from October 11 to 13 with sermons by Fr. Walter Grill, diocesan priest, native son of St. Alphonsus, and pastor of St. Pius X Church in Grandville. An open house was held October 27 for all denominations to join our Jubilee. Over 40 Redemptorists from all across the nation were expected to attend.

Fr. Herbert A. Seifert's 50th Jubilee, September 5, 1961

The new liturgy of the Mass began at St. Alphonsus Parish on November 29, 1964. The altar and priest faced the people. The Mass now used more English and the readings were proclaimed by lay people.

By 1965, the church (which seats 700) was accommodating approximately 3,500 people at the six weekend Masses. Weekday Masses had an attendance of about 200 adults, with double or triple that number depending on the holy day or season.

The Feast of St. Gerard, October 16, 1965, saw the first high Mass in English at the 9:30 Mass. It was also during this time that one parishioner remembers, "The choir director at the time quit when Fr. Langton told her to sing the vernacular Mass. She said, 'It's not going to last—this English Mass.' She just hated it. She wouldn't do it. But Fr. Langton was determined we were going to the vernacular. So she up and quit."

President Kennedy was assassinated in Dallas, Texas, November 22, 1963.

The plans for the new St. Alphonsus School were detailed in The Grand Rapids Press on January 18, 1964. "The multi-level addition to St. Alphonsus School will replace the old two-story and three-story wings between Carrier and Leonard Street NE, leaving a wing on Lafayette Avenue. constructed in 1957, to which the new school addition

Senator John F. Kennedy campaigning for president in Grand Rapids October 1960.

will be built. When completed, the school will have 24 classrooms, with two unfinished rooms for future use. To be constructed on varying levels, a three-story wing will house a library, an all-purpose room, cafeteria, kitchen, and various meeting rooms and offices as well as classrooms." "A memorial to John F. Kennedy is included with the scheduled dedication of the gym-multipurpose room included in the St. Alphonsus' School plans." "Designed by VanAllsburg and Koprowski, local architects, the general contract has been awarded to Owen-Ames-Kimball Co. The addition will be of brick construction."

Demolition of the old school building on Leonard Street began on March 16, 1964. One person's memory recalls, "The school went up in two phases. The first wing built was the East one that hooks to the one that stretches out toward Lafayette St. When they started the second phase, they started tearing the school down from Leonard to Carrier. The east wing of the School built in 1957 cost $224,000, with

The new St. Alphonsus School

PODIATRIST POINTS THE WAY!

One arm outstretched, the other waving traffic forward, a smile, a friendly nod, and an "Okay, folks, come on, let's go!" That's how I remember "Officer" Leiber. Sunday mornings, rain or shine, in the middle of the intersection, moving the traffic on the corner of Lafayette and Carrier Streets. He successfully decreased congestion and helped get the parishioners at St. Alphonsus out of the parking lot and safely on their way home between the Masses starting every hour.

Beryl Leiber was so much more though. An actor, and an inventor, Doctor Leiber was a podiatrist for more than 50 years, providing kind and compassionate care. He was an avid outdoorsman, taught the first hunter's safety course in West Michigan, and taught firearms safety for the Sheriff's Department. "Officer" Leiber taught safety to children as the first West Michigan "Crime Dog" McGruff.

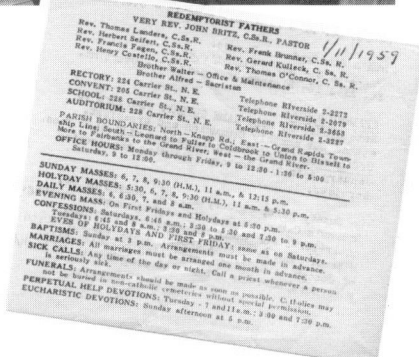

Doctor Leiber, his wife, Anne, and their children, Carole and Dennis (now Judge Leiber) were members of St. Alphonsus for several years after moving from Chicago.

Thank you, Doctor Leiber, for your years of service!

The St. Alphonsus School east wing

the cost of the new School construction costing $440,000. They took the kids from that school and ran them half days. The other kids went the other half days. That way, they could get them all in. They only lost a week in the fall." Another concession to the building process was that St. Alphonsus did not have a first grade for that year.

Fr. Oelerich, C.Ss.R. wrote to the parents August 21, 1964:

Dear Parents:

I'm sure you join with us all in the excitement of opening our new school. With our expansion, Saint Alphonsus School will open its doors to over 950 children—the largest enrollment ever in the parish's history, making ours the largest parochial school in the Diocese. This should make us grateful to God for His flood of graces over these past 75 years. 'Unless God builds the house, he who builds does so in vain.'

Although three-fourths of our school building will be completely new, we do not wish to lose any of the old spirit. We ask you to help continue the inspiring tradition of cooperative, loyal, and deep interest in our school, our children and our parish. Many of our present parents are happily numbered among the graduates of Saint Alphonsus.

By this letter we hope to praise and thank the vast majority of our parents who have done so well. However, when dealing with some 400 families having children in school, one is not surprised to find a few "defaults." We hope that these happened through oversight and were not deliberate. The points of concern are the following items:
1. Fees — for tuition ($30.00 per family)
2. Playground supervision — $1.50 fine for each absence (fee for a substitute)
3. Home and School meetings the request: "attend at least one meeting."

Thanking the past faculties, officers of the Home and School, and parents for all they have done, I promise to beg God's blessing on you and our present faculty, officers and parents.

All Heaven Bless You,
Your Children and Homes

Father R. Oelerich, C.Ss.R.
(School Moderator)

St. Alphonsus School held an Open House on Sunday, November 15, 1964 from 1:00 to 8:00 P.M.

The enrollment for 1965 was 889 students in 24 classrooms. There were approximately 37 students per classroom. The students were taught by 17 Dominican Sisters, 2 of whom teach music, and 9 lay teachers. One Sister was a full-time principal. Teacher qualifications were the same as for public school. The same classrooms were used on Sundays for Catechism classes for approximately 400 public school children, taught by lay people (members of the Confraternity of Christian Doctrine). St. Alphonsus School had a hot lunch program, its own school bus, library, and athletic program. Who could forget the peanut butter and honey sandwiches on one slice of white and one slice of wheat bread lovingly prepared through the decades by Mrs. Shangraw, Mrs. Eno, and Mrs. Cave? Or how every day at noon, when the church bells would ring, even the older boys would stop whatever they were doing on the playground and say the Angelus.

Sue Kosten recalled feeling so sorry for our St. Alphonsus maintenance man and bus driver, Mr. Bockheim, because he was deaf. She later learned that his "hearing aid" was really part of his transistor radio. He was listening to the ballgame.

Blessing the new school cornerstone, November 15, 1964

The St. Al's dances were very popular in the sixties! "Back in Father Oelerich's time, we had a tremendous youth club. The kids had a lot of fun at their monthly dances. That gym was filled with them. It was at the time when they had those psychedelic, bright flashing lights (strobe lights). The kids did all those dances. Some of them were kind of objectionable. Father Oelerich put a stop to that too. But they always had a lot of fun. It was a wonderful organization." Teens from all over the city came to the St. Al's dances. The St. Alphonsus Youth Club purchased all the shrubbery and decorated the parish grounds.

The struggle for civil rights was a big part of the nation's history in the sixties. The same was true in Grand Rapids. The proposed "Open Housing" ordinance in the 2nd Ward caused quite a stir. Part of the affected area included the park across from Mary Waters Park on Lafayette Ave. Sr. Emma and Sr. Marie Michael became the moving spirits behind the integration movement in the St. Alphonsus neighborhood. They arranged a meeting involving a variety of people to help our neighbors understand the topic. More than 70 people attended a meeting held at the church on November 15, 1967, as reported in The Grand Rapids Press. Dr. Lewis Clingman, chairman of the Aquinas College History Department, began to explore the myths and fears surrounding integration.

Laying the new school cornerstone, November 15, 1964

Rev. Francis Novak, pastor, opened with, "The purpose of these meetings is to discover ways and means of putting over the idea of integration on a local level so that it is agreeable with the people." Fr. Novak said the people of the 2nd Ward "have more good will than it has been credited with." The fears were "enhanced by a great deal of ignorance." The meetings attempted to overcome the fears.

Change was coming and St. Alphonsus Parish tried to be a conduit.

CHAPTER 8
THE 1970S: TURBULENT TIMES

Change is difficult, especially within a space we think of in many ways as home. Many people had many opinions with each renovation and redecorating plan for St. Alphonsus Church. Dramatic changes were in store following Vatican II which ushered in the general feeling for the need to modernize buildings. The city of Grand Rapids made many changes and at the same time plans were being made for changes at St. Alphonsus. Integration and subsidized housing had come to the neighborhood and many people were uneasy and unhappy with that. Many of the proposals for the modernization of the Church would eliminate many of the comfortable, feel like home decorations in the church. The angels on the ceiling running the length of the church would be gone, as would the apostles in the transepts and the big side altars and confessionals, and the communion

St. Joseph's Shrine

rail repurposed by the time the renovation would be completed. There were several very heated meetings under four pastors—Fr. Novak, Fr. Quinn, Fr. Monroe, and Fr. Hillary—before decisions were finalized. One meeting ended with the pastor essentially saying, "This is going to happen! Get used to it."

Here are some of the memories, notes and letters describing the very controversial renovation in 1978 from the Centennial Jubilee booklet.

1978 Redemptorist Shrine

"At that particular time, when we were first discussing renovating the church, Fr. Monroe was pastor. And they had some people meet, and they made some suggestions. Before we got through with this thing, we had 19 pages of things we wanted to do."

1978 Mary's Shrine

"Being like we are, we didn't all agree, and it caused quite a commotion. They formed a committee, had another meeting, and elected a second committee. The fellow that was chairman of the second committee was going to run it democratically."

"They had that meeting downstairs, and they brought this priest in. The only decoration pictures he had were of Lutheran churches, and some people were uptight. You heard a guy over there who has a son who's a priest and four brothers. He got up and said, We don't have to go to the Lutheran's. Let them come to us."

SPECIAL BLESSING CELEBRATION

Article from the West Michigan Catholic

In the midst of all of the turmoil, the Parish celebrated an awesome event. Three of their "sons" were ordained on June 2, 1978. They returned to celebrate their "first Mass" together at their home Parish of St. Alphonsus. And what a joyous celebration it was with its breathtaking reverence at the Mass and the beautiful harmony of the many Redemptorist priests who attended. "It was absolutely awesome!" "Bill Bueche, Tom Santa and myself (Gary Ziuraitis) had our first mass together on the 4th or 5th of June in 1978. We didn't want to tax the resources of the parish for **three** First Masses, so we had a combined concelebrated celebration and reception. It was quite nice and a nice way (unknown to us at the time) to end the long Redemptorist string of ordinations—until Aaron Meszaros has his turn (2016)."

Fathers Ziuraitis, Santa and Bueche celebrate Mass

Church Renovation Report from the Renovation Committee, October 1978

St. Alphonsus Parish is a living and dynamic parish community—the proof is in the concern, care and support of our loyal parishioners. You asked that in our renovation efforts we preserve the dignity and heritage of this great parish, yet foster a greater feeling of community. We're sure that when you see our newly decorated church you will agree with all the parishioners and visiting priests that it is truly a beautiful and proper place for worship.

The first thing you will notice is the bright, warm colors; the feeling of elegance; even the angels high above the new altar platform seem to be smiling with pleasure. The Caen stone colored pillars and walls enhance the Gothic beauty of our church.

The cleaned and repaired stained glass windows glow with a new beauty all their own. Our restored stations help accent the brightness of our outstanding windows.

We've heard so much favorable response about the seating arrangement in the gym that we know you'll like the seating arrangement in the church—three wide aisles, and seating on three sides of the altar, with easy access from the front door or the side doors.

The changes begin, scaffolding, 1978

The large marble baldachin in all its majesty blends much better into the architecture of the church and is a fitting and dignified canopy for the reservation of the Blessed Sacrament.

The Communion rail will once again receive full use as it supports those kneeling at our various shrines.

We did put in the restrooms that most everyone agreed we needed so badly. They're in the vestibule tucked into the corners by the old baptistery. The baptistery will continue to be used as a bride's room and a vestry.

We have proceeded with the construction of vestibules for our side doors. These should insure the comfort of the congregation and help preserve the heat produced by our upgraded heating system. The upgrading of our heating system will also make our redecoration last longer.

We rewired the entire church to meet modern electrical codes and put in new lighting. Now we have plenty of light to read by, and also have great flexibility in light control. This will enable us to emphasize certain areas of the church on occasion and also establish any desired atmosphere for our various services. The new lamps are also easier to rebulb than our previous ones.

We are still researching the upgrading of our sound system, and also the design of our sanctuary furnishings.

We originally projected the cost of this renovation at $500,000, but unlike most projects, this one has been reduced to just under $450,000. We were only able to do this by postponing the ventilation system, the commons-cry room wall, and the organ.

Through the generosity of our parishioners, we already have $353,000 pledged. This, combined with our building fund reserve of $120,000 made the whole effort feasible. Because such a large number of our people have been willing to sacrifice, we see no problem in paying off our indebtedness in three to five years.

Our loan is being cosigned in part by the diocese and in part by the Redemptorist Congregation. A more complete financial report will be given later.

We wish to thank those who have advanced your pledge payments and those of you who are making your pledge payments on time. We hope and pray you can continue to do so, and if any others can pay sooner, it makes your pledge more valuable because of the high interest rates on borrowed money.

If any of you were unable to make a pledge earlier and now wish to make one, just leave your name at the rectory and you will be given an opportunity.

We are still hoping to reopen the church in March, but a lot depends upon the arrival of our carpeting and pews.

Many of you that have been over to peek at the work to date have been quite enthusiastic, but you are only getting a hint of the beauty that will be there when it is finished. With all the glowing reports, we don't know how anyone can stay away, but for those that do, you will not be disappointed. Even though the church will seat as many as before, we're sure that it will be much harder to get a seat when everyone has seen our church and participated in our liturgies!

Keep praying for the renovation and for the unity and spiritual renewal of our Parish.

The Steering Committee

Tom Deschaine, Fr. Mike Hillary, Harry Mika, Mary Anne Romanowski, Bob Stritzinger

Church had a re-opening liturgy on May 20, 1979.

CHAPTER 9
THE LAST 25 YEARS

The last 25 years have brought many changes to both our physical plant as well as to our community. The physical changes are the easiest to identify. Many of the organizations and events that occurred are forever a part of the rich history of an ever evolving parish. We will try to identify those that have happened or concluded within the last 25 years with the

Parish Picnic with Fr. Andy, The Hormuths, the Knapes, Barb Vincent, Mary McMahon, and Dee Kamsickas — mid 1980s

disclaimer that we know we are missing some pretty important things. Many of the stories will be told in depth in other areas of this book. However, here is our attempt to identify some of the major milestones.

THE CONVENT

In the late 1980s with the dwindling number of Dominican Sisters living in the convent, the decision was made to move their residence to the "Shangraw house." Those walls carry a lot of memories of the sisters for example, the piano studio with Sr. Humilitas. Their legacy lives on with the hundreds of students the sisters taught and mentored. The convent built in the 1940s had become too large and the upkeep became too much for the few sisters who were still living there. Some of them, like Sr. Anselma Weber and Sr. Theodore Mary, were ready to move back to the Dominican Mother House. So Sr. Olga Mizzi, Sr. Roberta Hefferon, and Sr. Jean Milhaupt moved into the "house across the parking lot" where they would remain until 2012. Meanwhile Fr. Jack Dowd, the Creston Neighborhood Association (CNA) as well as the Housing Development began the process of turning the convent into an affordable housing for senior citizens. The extra space in the lower level of the building allowed for the offices of the CNA, and the Parish Food and Clothing Pantry to be relocated there. You'll find their individual stories elsewhere in the book.

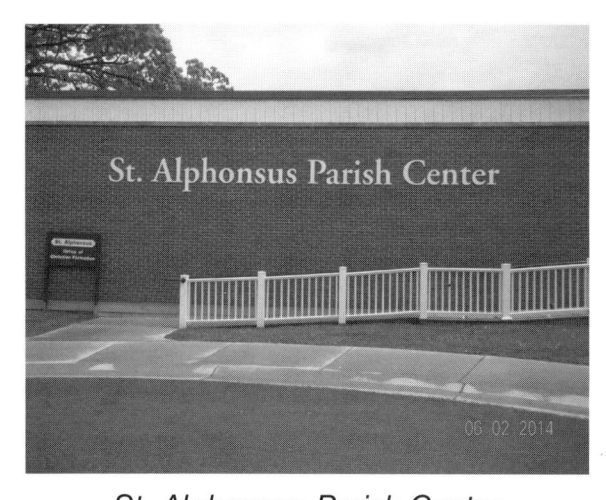

St. Alphonsus Parish Center

THE PARISH SCHOOL

The Parish School in the 1980s and early 1990s was experiencing a resurgence of sorts. The enrollment moved upward with the creation of a preschool program during the 1980/1981 school year. As the 1980s progressed, enrollment topped out around 400 students under the leadership of Mr. Phillip Haack and staff. Funding for the school continued to be a challenge. Out of these challenges (as happened so many times in history) came some wonderful community building fundraisers.

Parish Picnic with Bob Thiel and Tom Deschaine

PARISH LENTEN FISH FRY

The Fish Fry's were developed and launched in the mid to late '80s during Fr. Jack Dowd's time as Pastor as a fundraiser for the school. Who could forget that first year? Dale McDonald and

Parish Breakfast crew

his group of "fearless fishers" had only three that first season. The delicious "fish recipe" was developed by Mike Duba and family. The weather was horrible all three nights that they were held, and folks were picked up who were fearful of driving. And remember Fr. Doug Klukken dressed up as a shark? You had to appreciate his love for our parish that he'd take all that ribbing! The yearly Lenten event is quickly approaching 30 years. Tons of fish and thousands of customers have created quite a legacy in our parish and certainly in the community! Thanks to many hundreds of volunteers and chairpersons like Steve Allen, Linda Parker, Juli Lillis, and Bob Thiel who have coordinated the action.

ARTS AND CRAFTS BAZAARS

The Saturday after Thanksgiving became quite the event for the school. Hundreds of crafters would buy a spot in the gym, in the cafeteria and up the hallways to participate in one of the top craft bazaars in the area. Thousands of dollars were raised through the '90s that allowed for staff development for the teachers in the school. Remember all of the early elementary teachers going to New Orleans to learn Workshop Way? Not to be slighted, the Middle School teachers headed to Wisconsin to learn how to implement the directives from the Carnegie Report on Middle Schools. Led by Miss Mary Wysocki, they came back and established a wonderful model program that then spread and was emulated by many.

PARISH FOUNDATION AND ENDOWMENT

Both of these were "born" out of need to find additional funding for the parish and the school. Their individual stories are highlighted in the book. The Foundation was established in 1984. The School Development Committee in the '80s led into the Educational Endowment in the '90s. Together these two permanent funds will continue to be vital resources for our Parish.

ST. AL'S NEIGHBORHOOD STREET NAMES

"THEN AND NOW"

The village of Grand Rapids was incorporated in 1837. In the following decade there was substantial growth. The village then became the City of Grand Rapids in 1850. At that time St. Al's didn't exist and the area was the "way north" end of the established boundaries. It was mostly woods, orchards and farmlands.

Fast forward to 1888 when the Parish of St. Alphonsus was being established. Here is a list of the street names then and how we know them now.

The Shipman Coal Company that stands today as the Choo Choo Grill!

Now	Then	Year Changed
Plainfield Ave	Plainfield Rd	1873
Curtis St	Chubb	1877
Brenner Ct	Crabapple Alley	1888
Matthews Ct	Colfax Alley	1891
Knapp St	Ninth St	1892
Shanahan Ct	King Court	1892
Dale St	Second St	1892
Travis St	Third St	1892
Ann St	Fifth St	1892
Burr Oak St	Seventh St	1892
Spencer St	Madison St	1899
Maude Ave	Forrest St	1899
Dean St	Hazel St	1899
Queen Ave	King Ct	1899
Monroe Ave	Canal St	1912
Page St	Crescent Ct	1912
Berlin Place	Briggs Place	1912
Carman Ave	Henrietta St	1920
Buffalo Ave	Perry Ave	1920
Cole Ave	Stuard Ave	1928
Emerald Ave	Ryn Court	1928
Paris Ave	Christ St	1938
Houseman Ave	Armstrong Ave	1938

Used with permission from "the rapidian."
An article authored by Michael Page.

Festival Country Store

PARISH FESTIVALS

What a fun, long history these had. They were a source of additional funding for the Parish, but more than that they were a weekend long chance for the community to come together as family. The preparations started months ahead of time. What fond memories we have of Fr. Oelerich and Fr. Comer

Black jack dealer at Festival – Terry Farrey

driving to Chicago to "pick up supplies." Remember the school children competing classroom against classroom to see who could bring in enough can goods to win the class prize? These donations along with a chicken or two would be added to bushel baskets for "The Country Store"…… surely one of the favorite games of chance. The kids would be rewarded with a carnival of their own on Friday afternoon where everyone went home a winner. Some of the attractions were the Chicken dinner, sweet treats and dressed dolls at the Ladies of the Holy Family booth, plus the blackjack tables and bingo. The weekend was full of fun. By the end of the '90s, the time came to end the run. But still today we hear… Could we just revisit it "like the old days"!

Festival games with the Keeney's

THE AUCTION

This began in one of the last years of the Parish Festival. A tent was rented for the front lawn of the rectory and if memory serves us correctly netted around $1,000 for the parish. The hot items that first year

The first Auction and the Holy Water font!

were pews and holy water fonts from the Convent which was in the process of being rehabbed. After the first year, the Auction stood on it's own and grew and grew till it was a "themed event" in February raising lots of dollars for the Endowment Fund. Who didn't look forward to "Mardi Gras" to kick off the Lenten season? Many a trip was made to the Voodoo Lounge! Paddles were raised for dinners, bikes, fishing trips, and art. The menus and desserts were so memorable. The Auction went on hiatus a few years ago—but who knows, maybe it will return some day.

Mardi Gras Auction workers, Robin Dupuie and Laura Hummel Stawasz

Emcee Dan Fortier

HIS LAST DAYS

We were blessed with this wonderful cantata presented on Palm Sunday and Good Friday by our Parish Music Department every year in the late 1980s and the 1990s. Hundreds of hours of preparation and practice brought forth this moving musical masterpiece reflecting on the Passion of our Lord. Thousands of people from the parish and the city would pack the pews on Palm Sunday and on Good Friday for the highly anticipated musical service. The

Choir circa 1990s

talent consisted of musicians who all called St. Alphonsus their spiritual home. Michelle Ogren and Paula Annis were the directors who blessed us with this wonderful ministry.

The list goes on into infinity: the Parish Missions every two years, Homecoming Weekend, the Wall of Fame, the "over 35" men's softball leagues, the New Years Eve parties, the funeral lunches, the Greeter program, the Renew program, Thanksgiving dinners, St. Patrick's Day parties, church cleaning bee's, cooking classes, parish breakfasts, Vacation Bible School, Interfaith Gatherings and St. Gerard Sewing Guild. So many, many more groups that we are sure we are missing them. Hopefully some of these will jog memories and reminiscing for you. Traditionally we don't do a very good job of recording these groups and events! They are part of the fabric of the everyday life of a parish. And then an opportunity like the 125th comes along and we wish we had "written it down" or talked to our Mom, Dad, or "Aunt Louise" more to get the stories that they have. Missed opportunities!

Steve Angrisano with the Parish Priests at his Mission in April

CHAPTER 10
THE PROUD TRADITION

St. Alphonsus Parish School has been an integral part of parish life since its inception in 1889. The emphasis of St. Al's Parish School has focused around the following areas.

SPIRITUAL DEVELOPMENT

As an extension of the church and the home, St. Al's School emphasized both the importance of learning about our Catholic faith and the importance of worship to the students. In the "olden days" students found themselves beginning each school day with attendance at Mass. In the 1970s and onward, students attended Mass weekly at 9:00 AM and also on special holy days. Each class took turns in preparing the liturgy—selecting the readings and the songs to be sung. Students also took on the roles of readers who proclaimed God's word

The 1977-78 Faculty. How many can you name?

while others—both girls and boys—volunteered as altar servers.

Mrs. Anne Harpold, our last principal

In addition to the weekly Masses, students received daily classroom religious instruction. Religion classes were considered part of the core curriculum. Included in this curriculum was instruction in the reception of various sacraments.

During our final school year, our pastor, Father Denis Ryan, sought another way to involve the eighth graders in their spiritual development. He commissioned each eighth grader to become a Eucharistic minister. These eighth graders served at every school Mass with great reverence and dignity.

ACADEMIC DEVELOPMENT

St. Alphonsus Parish School provided an education that enabled their students to grow academically and to successfully compete with students from other schools. A number of St. Al's graduates went on to become valedictorians and salutatorians from both Catholic and public high schools.

St. Al's became a leader in implementing new programs that fostered student learning. One example of this leadership came in the form of a K–3 program called Workshop Way which stressed academic achievement while also assisting students in developing responsibility, life skills, creativity, and becoming self starters.

Dan Duba, Bob Tobin and Fr. Tom "consulting" about set up for a fundraiser.

Graduation girls from St. Al's eighth grade 1967

Another innovative program that was established at St. Al's focused on the middle school students. This program was an outgrowth of a study conducted by the Carnegie Institute. This educational think tank recognized a need for middle schools to focus not only on students achieving high academic success, but also on recognizing individual students as unique persons.

Students' academic experiences also included musical training and exposure to technology.

ATHLETIC DEVELOPMENT

The importance of providing athletic opportunities was also a strong component of school. St. Al's sponsored teams for both girls and boys enabling students in various grades to learn how to play a particular sport and to become more physically fit. Volleyball, baseball, softball, cheerleading, basketball, football, and soccer teams were formed.

SOCIAL DEVELOPMENT

While learning flourished at St. Al's, students found many opportunities for fun also. Some of the social experiences students had were as follows.

VIP (Very Important Person) Days were always a favorite. Students invited a "very important person" in their life to attend Mass with them and then spend the morning revisiting what a day in the life of a student was like.

Fr. Richard Quinn and Mr. Phillip Haack at the "Homecoming Weekend

The "Wall of Fame" was another important part of school. Students enjoyed finding Wall of Fame pictures of family members who graduated from St. Al's while adults found this to be a wonderful stroll down memory lane. Generations of family members who attended St. Al's are represented in these pictures.

Juli O'Rourke-Lillis and Don Nugent preparing another gourmet meal

Regina (Patin) Clouse and Jacob Clouse staffing a Scan and Pray for the Archives

Days when students met in Angel Groups (groups composed of one student from every grade) were always highly anticipated school days where students performed various service projects around the parish.

Super Buddies (groups paired from one grade level to another grade level) was another school group that furthered a community feeling among students.

THE FINAL SCHOOL YEAR

The 2007–2008 school year was a year filled with many mixed emotions for students, faculty, parents, priests, and parishioners of St. Al's. Bishop Walter Hurley—in consultation with the priests—decided to consolidate our school with the schools of Blessed Sacrament, St. Isidore, and St. Jude to form our new parish school of All Saints Academy (ASA). ASA would serve the students and families of these four parishes at two campuses—the Diamond Avenue Campus (former Blessed Sacrament School) housing preschool through fourth grade and the 4 Mile Campus (former St. Jude School) housing fifth through eighth grade.

During our final year, St. Al's School decided to celebrate our existence and our history. A committee—

Our final year at St. Alphonsus School was spent praying, learning, and celebrating together. The memories that were formed that year—and those formed over a one hundred year plus period of time when the school existed—will remain a major influence on hundreds of youngsters and their families.

St. Al's students, Nick Hulswitt, Sarah Eyk and Audrey Genautis

The Dream Team—was formed to ensure that our traditions of faith, scholarship, and parish belonging would be emphasized. This team consisted of parents and faculty and was spear headed by Mrs. Linda Parker. "The Dream Team" formulated many opportunities for students, faculty, and parents to celebrate our roots while looking forward to the future.

Peanut butter and honey sandwiches with Betty Eno and Bonnie Cave

Kevin and Abby Lyons

THE STORY OF THE CROSS

Each and every class from 1889 until 2008 left their mark on our Parish and on our Hearts.

One of the goals during our last year of having the School on our physical campus was to HAVE FUN and celebrate with joy and gladness that these kids also left their legacy. Thus the creation of the School Cross. Our theme for the year was

"WE REMEMBER, WE CELEBRATE, WE BELIEVE!"

Each student, faculty member, staff member, and priest designed a ceramic tile that was used to form a large St. Al's School cross that resides in the stairwell near the elevator. Each tile—designed by the individual student, staff member, or priest—depicted something important in that person's life. This cross was blessed and dedicated at the 125th opening Mass and dinner celebration on September 28, 2013. The Cross joins the Wall of Fame in becoming a permanent reminder of all the students and staff who walked the halls of St. Al's for 120 years!

The proud tradition of St. Al's students continues today at our "new" Parish School, All Saints Academy.

CHEERS FOR THE CARA CLUB

Parishioners who have been involved with St. Al's all know of the important role the CARA Club has played in our parish. The CARA Club (Catholic Athletics and Related Activities) was established at St. Al's on June 8, 1956. The first president was Charles Page and Father Barton was their religious leader. Records show the following men were members of the initial CARA Club:

Bernard D'Orazio	Jim Wallacker	Tony Lamonaco
Walter Thiel	Ed Mead	Jerry Foley
Ted Lascari	Wilford Bohr	Herb Hussey
Ed Gibson	Gerald Schildroth	Warren Griffin
Bud Lindeman	Norm Schumaker	Chuck Stevens
John Milanowski	Bernie Murray	

On September 21, 1959 Dave VanDyke's name was submitted for membership. Dave's joining the CARA Club was the beginning of a long association of generosity from him. Dave owned Prep Sports and was a huge contributor for the rest of the history of sports at St. Al's.

The CARA Club functioned in many capacities within the parish. For example, they staffed various festivals, bingos, purchased computer software, and even covered the cost of insurance for students of our school. When the orphans of St. John's Home needed transportation to attend various activities, the CARA Club members stepped up and provided rides for these children. When the parish needed a group to run the church youth

Two generations of the Alphonsus Hillary family at a golf outing.

77

group, the CARA Club members agreed to expand this program under the guidance of Father Barton. Sewing classes also came under the umbrella of the CARA Club. Beginning in 1959, the wives of CARA Club members ran these classes for over 100 girls with the CARA Club purchasing and maintaining the sewing machines. January of 1961 found a new proposal for the CARA Club's consideration. They were asked and agreed to begin publishing a paper called the "Green & White." This paper would help raise funds to support the sports programs at St. Al's School. In November of 1965, they planned the first of many popular "record dances" that attracted young people from all across the city. Cost of admission to these dances was 50 cents per person.

Two stellar members of Cara Club, Benny D'Orazio and Frank DeMario… inseparable.

One of the CARA Club's first fund-raisers was an autumn ham dinner. Tickets to this dinner were $1 for adults and 50 cents for children. The profits from this first dinner were shared with 10% given to the Catholic Daughters, 60% donated to the parish general fund, and the remaining 30% kept by the CARA Club.

An additional venture sponsored by the CARA Club was the annual New Year's Eve dance. The first dance was held in 1957. After all expenses were paid, a profit of $40 was made. This dance became a yearly event for many years.

Bernie Murray, Charlie Page and Tony Krenselewski setting up for "something" for the millionth time!

However, the CARA Club was most prominently known for their dedication to the athletic programs of our school. They sponsored teams of bowling, football, baseball, softball, basketball, volleyball, soccer, and cheerleading. In addition to paying entry fees for each of the teams, they also paid for uniforms and equipment for the teams. Initial costs for team uniforms were modest—$8 per uniform—but as time went on these costs increased with the CARA Club always footing the bill for each team. Coaches for each team were also recruited from interested parents and parishioners.

Cara Club members hard at work manning the pop & popcorn. Doug McKay, Tom Hummel and Pat Byrnes

During the existence of St. Al's School, the CARA Club also funded many structural improvements. In 1964 a new school was constructed—including a new gym. A concession stand, new bleachers (costing $2.560) and a pop machine (costing $279) were generously funded by the CARA Club. As the years went on, they purchased an ice machine at a cost of $2,100. In 1986 carpet was installed on the gym walls at a cost of $1,464. In 1992-1993 the CARA Club shared the cost of replacing the floor in the gym and cafeteria.

Eddie Gibson working Bingo

There were numerous adult volunteers who offered their time and talents as coaches for the various teams. Others found themselves volunteering in various capacities at basketball games and tournaments hosted by our parish school. These tournaments—known as The Tournament of Champions—

required 30 to 35 volunteers to assist with this activity and the Cara Club members always filled these positions.

One of the dedicated CARA Club members was Tom Barnes. Tom's affiliation with the CARA Club began in 1971 when he was hired as a teacher at St. Al's School. During his first year at St. Al's, he began serving as a liaison between school and the Cara Club. This position then evolved into becoming the athletic director of the school. Tom's dedication to the Catholic sports program reached beyond St. Al's. He also was a liaison and later president of the Grand Rapids Area Athletic Council. Over the years, Tom coached the St. Al's girls' softball teams and the boys' baseball teams. Tom also scheduled all of the many basketball tournaments St. Al's hosted. Tom's dedication to our students and their athletic development was monumental and he will always be remembered for his devotion to the students and the Cara Club.

Norm & Peg Schumaker, the best "ticket sellers" ever!

Mike & Scott Schumaker volunteering at a game at Festival

CHAPTER 11
REDEMPTORISTS AND ST. ALPHONSUS PARISH

Who was St. Alphonus Ligouri?

He was born of noble parents in Naples Italy. He was destined by his lineage and by his father's plan for him to have a law career. At the young age of 16 he was made a Doctor of Laws and admitted to the Bar. A brilliant future lay before him. He passed his youthful years in deeds of devotion and charity. And still his life seemed to be laid in the family circle.

But God had other designs for Alphonsus. First a vocation to the priesthood and then to found a religious order. He followed through trials and doubts, hardships and sacrifices that would have daunted a weaker soul. He achieved the work God gave him to do. He founded the Congregation of the Most Holy Redeemer in 1732.

Circa 1940s

He became one of God's noblemen and reached an eminent holiness of

Fr. George Liesveld

At the age of 66, the Holy Father made him Bishop of St. Agatha of the Goths—a charge he fulfilled with great prudence and wisdom and charity for 12 years. Forced by exhaustion and illness to resign, he returned as a humble religious to his congregation and died at the age of 91.

Seldom do we see in the life of a saint such a combination of scholar, missionary, bishop, Founder of an order and a contemplative.

life; the eloquent pleader became a missionary whose words were irresistible and brought thousands of souls to God. The royal counselor-to-be became God's chosen one to lead a band of men to seek out the poor and abandoned and in imitation of Our Redeemer to preach the Gospel to them.

Fr. Tom Donaldson, 25th, 2002

The Church declared him a Saint in 1839 and declared him a Doctor of the church in 1871.

THE ROAD TO ST. AL'S GRAND RAPIDS

From the beginnings of the Redemptorists in Italy in 1732 to the entire world they serve today............

Fr. Chuck Beierwaltes

The first step in the spread of the Redemptorist Congregation was the entrance of the order beyond the Alps by St. Clement Hofbauer. His moves forced upon him by persecuting governments, from Austria to Poland, to Prussia, to Bavaria and Switzerland. Divine Providence was used to carry the seed over the greater part of Europe. Before his death St. Clement had visions of establishing the Redemptorists in America. This dream was realized under his successor, Ven. Joseph Passerat, C.Ss.R. who sent the first Fathers to America.

Fr. Denis Ryan

On June 20, 1832, six Redemptorists, three Fathers and three brothers landed in New York. Little did they know of the work that lay before them and for a number of years, they pioneered in various cities beginning in Cincinnati, Detroit, Green Bay and Rochester. Poverty and hardship were all a part of their work. Many times they thought of giving up. But as new men arrived it became possible to establish the first real community in Pittsburgh in the year 1839. From that point on it grew fast in establishments and in work.

Class of '58

Forty years later, in 1875 provinces were established.

A generous benefactor gave the then Bishop Henry Joseph Richter $60,000 to "purchase grounds and erect suitable buildings for an

Fr. Turk Rooney's Jubilee

Community of Grand Rapids, Michigan, 1900
Left to right: Rev. Frs. Barrett, Cronin, White, and Urben.

Top Row - L. to R. Bro. Andrew Patin, C.Ss.R.
Rev. Edward Comer, C.Ss.R.
Rev. Richard Quinn, C.Ss.R. - Pastor
Bottom Row - L. to R. Rev. John Farnik, C.Ss.R.
Rev. Clair Collins, C.Ss.R.
Bro. James Bohr, C.Ss.R.

Top left: Redemptorist Community 1900
Right: Redemptorist Community 1960
Bottom left: Redemptorist Community 1975

July 12, 1993

orphan asylum in the city. At this same time Bishop Richter knew that the Cathedral Parish of St. Andrews was overcrowded and he decided to divide it and form a new parish in the North End. With the $60,000 he bought enough land to build not only the asylum but also a church, school and other necessary parochial buildings. The vision was well conceived but who was to be intrusted with the new and difficult undertaking? His desire was to hand over this to one of the many religious orders of clergy. After some negotiating, he succeeded in obtaining the consent of the Redemptorist Fathers to assume control. The building of the orphanage was well underway before the first two Redemptorists arrived in the latter part of August 1888.

REV. MARK VAN CORP, C.Ss.R.
(Missionary)

REV. AUGUST T. PETERS, C.Ss.R.
(Missionary)

The Denver Province was established in June of 1996 when the former St. Louis Province (established in 1875) and the Oakland Province (established in 1952) merged to form one Province, later joined by the Vice-Province of New Orleans (established in 1952) in 2005. Over the years foreign missions had been established in Brazil (1943), in Thailand (1949), and in Nigeria (1987). In 2012 Thailand became an independent Province.

The Denver Province encompasses most of the continental United States stretching from Michigan to the West Coast. Members of the Province staff some 13 parishes and maintain three retreat centers, a publishing house (Liguori Publications), a health care center (St. Clement, where our elderly and infirm Redemptorists reside), and the Blessed Francis Seelos Shrine. Nearly 250 Redemptorist priests, brothers, and seminarians make up the Denver Province.

Fr. Dalton's 25th Jubilee, July 1, 1951

Fr. Tom Danielson, Anne Andrew and Matthew Lepech

THE LEGACY (HISTORY) OF PAGE ST. AND "VOCATION ALLEY"

Excerpts taken from the Grand Rapids Press, April 25, 1987

In the past 60 years, at least 32 boys from this small neighborhood on the Northeast side of Grand Rapids have become Roman Catholic priests and brothers. Another dozen or so women from this area – on, or along Page Street have become nuns. Countless others have attended seminary or entered convents for varying period of time.

No one is quite sure why this two block long street has been the breeding ground for so many religious vocations. Some attribute it to the proximity of the church, some put it down to chance, and still others wonder if maybe God has had a hand in it all. Others jokingly say there must be something in the holy water.

While no one can say for sure whom…many attribute the wonderful influence of the Redemptorist priests and brothers who were frequent visitors to their parishioner's homes. Many a "Good Father" was seen walking down the streets that encompassed the Parish boundaries. Legendary families like the Miller's, who gave 4 boys and 1 daughter to the Redemptorist priesthood and to the Redemptoristine Sisters. Then there were the 4 Patin brothers, the 2 Grile boys, the Tobin's, the Hillary's, and the Earl's. What a rich harvest of vocations have come from this Parish. This story will live on, thanks to all of the blessings of Page Street!

Page Street Vocations

Rev. Frank Dalton
Rev. Richard Dalton

Rev. Donald Miller
Rev. Raymond Miller
Rev. Ernest Miller
Rev. Louis Miller

Rev. Bernard Tobin
Rev. Gerard Tobin

Bro. Leo Patin
Rev. Larry Patin

Bro. Andy Patin
Bro. Eugene Patin
Bro. Gerard Patin

Rev. Harry Grile
Rev. Patrick Grile

Rev. Joe Earl
Rev. Bob Earl

Rev. Mark VanGorp

Rev. Donald Schumaker

Rev. Gary Ziuraitis

Rev. Tom Page …
"the one who got away"

Redemptoristine Sr. Mary Margaret Miller

Vocation Alley — that's Page St.

By Chris Meehan
Press Religion Editor

They call it Vocation Alley.

In the past 60 years, at least 32 boys from this small neighborhood on the Northeast Side of Grand Rapids have become Roman Catholic priests or brothers.

Another dozen or so women from this area — on or along Page Street NE — have become nuns. And countless others have attended seminary or entered convents for varying periods of time.

No neighborhood residents have taken religious vows in the last few years, but this working class neighborhood in the shadow of St. Alphonsus Catholic Church, 224 Carrier NE, retains its reputation. People far and wide have heard, at one time or another, of Page Street and environs.

"Oh sure, Page Street is famous in our circles," said the Rev. Pete Schavitz, a vocations director for the Redemptorist Fathers and Brothers in St. Louis, Mo. "To have one guy come off a street is one thing, but to have this many is just amazing. It's really exceptional."

No one is quite sure why this two-block-long street has been the breeding ground for so many religious vocations. Some attribute it to the proximity of the church; some put it all down to chance; still others wonder if maybe God has had a hand in it all. Others jokingly say there must be something in the holy water.

What they do know, however, is that this neighborhood of modest, two-story homes has produced far more than its share of Catholic priests, brothers and nuns over the years.

"I think it was a mysterious combination of circumstances, natural and supernatural, that have called forth vocations from this street," said the Rev. Richard Quinn, St. Alphonsus' red-haired pastor.

"I don't think the boys and girls were breaking any new ground by entering the religious life. I think they were simply taking one of the honorable options open to them."

Regina Patin, whose four sons joined the Redemptorists, is among many neighborhood residents who, even after all of this time, remain a little perplexed by the Page Street phenomenon. She likes her neighborhood, but she never saw it as more important or more spiritual than any other.

"Maybe the finger of God has been on this street. What else could be the reason?" she asked.

Larry, her oldest son, is a missionary in Thailand. Her other boys — Leo, Gerry and Gene — work as religious brothers for the Redemptorists, formally known as the Congregation of the Most Sacred Redeemer.

To this day, she is hard-pressed to say why they all joined the ranks of the clergy.

"My boys were close to the priests and brothers at St. Al's," she said. "They loved to work up at the church; they liked that close connection. Maybe that's why they decided to go to seminary. I don't know."

Some people speculate that so many vocations have come from this area because of St. Alphonsus parishioners' prayers to the Blessed Mother.

Every Tuesday morning and evening more than 200 people kneel in the pews of this imposing, red-brick church for a novena dedicated entirely to fostering applications to the religious life.

"St. Al's has always had a family spirit, a very spiritual spirit," said Sister Roberta Hefferan, a Dominican nun who grew up near Page Street and is now a pastoral assistant.

"A lot of devotions are going on all of the time at this church. We take vocations very seriously.

"But she's not sure why God picked Page Street.

"That one is a mystery. You'd have to ask someone else about that," said Sister Hefferan.

While parishioners at St. Al's pray regularly for priests and nuns, the heyday for vocations coming from this parish, and especially from Page Street, is long past.

In fact, no one in recent years has left Page Street to join the Catholic clergy. There are now only two St. Alphonsus men in the seminary, and both are from another part of the parish.

"We're not getting nearly as many

see VOCATION, D2

The Rev. Thomas Page, associate pastor of St. Mary Magdalene parish in Kentwood, was first man to become diocesan priest from Page Street. His parents, Mr. and Mrs. Charles P. Page, are also sitting on front porch at 114 Page St. NE.

VOCATION
CONTINUED FROM D1

prospects anymore," said Quinn, the pastor. "It's a different culture today. Kids have so many more options. The days when you'd have four boys from one family going to seminary are probably long gone."

Coincidentally, the last local boy ordained a priest in this parish not only hails from Page Street, but bears the illustrious name of the street itself.

"I went into the seminary figuring I'd only stay a few months and ended up never coming out," said the Rev. Thomas Page, associate pastor at St. Mary Magdalene parish in Kentwood.

Page, whose great-great-great grandfather helped settle Grand Rapids, is the first man from Page Street to become a diocesan priest. All of the others joined the Redemptorist order, a group of missionary fathers that is based in Rome and operates the parish here.

As a diocesan priest, Page works in the Diocese of Grand Rapids. Since his ordination eight years ago, he has served as assistant pastor at several West Michigan churches.

Growing up on Page Street, he said, made it only natural for him to think of the priesthood as a career.

"It was a very Catholic area. It may be startling today for boys to decide to go to seminary, but it certainly wasn't when I was growing up," he recalled.

Up and down this street were homes where boys and girls had grown up to serve as priests and nuns. Such names as the Millers, Tobins, Patins, Hillaries and Earls were almost legendary and are even today spoken of with an almost reverential tone.

"There were constant reminders, some formal and some informal, that the religious life was there for us if only we wanted it," said Page.

The Rev. Louis Miller, a 74-year-old Redemptorist in the St. Louis, Mo., area, is one of four brothers who came off Page Street to become a priest. He also has a sister who is now head of a Redemptoristine order of sisters. "It is a real curious phenomenon," said Miller, who served for many years as editor of the Liguorian, a leading Catholic magazine. "I've often thought about why Page Street — what made that neighborhood so special?"

What he's come up with, after years of reflection, is that vocations are a result of personal attraction. Because he saw priests in his neighborhood, and particularly because his brothers were priests, Miller decided to try the seminary himself.

"I followed in the footsteps of others," he said. "As far back as I could remember, I wanted to be a priest. My mom and dad even tried to discourage me, but that didn't do any good."

The Rev. Mark VanGorp, who left Page Street more than 50 years ago to become a priest, agrees that attraction is the key. He recalls how the Redemptorist fathers used to fill his head with stories about working for God in far-off lands.

"They made it sound like the kind of life I'd like to lead," said VanGorp, a retired priest who served parishes all over the country and worked as a chaplain in the South Pacific during World War II.

"I've never regretted going in. I've had some tough times, but who hasn't? I'm glad for the vocation I got back on Page Street."

Vocations are plunging these days, not only on Page Street but all across the country. The Redemptorists now have about 5,000 priests around the world. Years ago there were more than 6,000.

"We're at a time of great change in this country, a time when a lot of the old values just aren't seen as important; family ties are looser," said Louis Miller. "There's a secularization, a moving away from the devotional life. The priesthood no longer seems like the thing to be part of."

Today, Page Street looks much like other aging city neighborhoods. Some homes have overgrown front yards; a few are in need of paint. And Catholics, who used to own nearly every home on the street, now share the neighborhood with people from Protestant churches, as well as those who have no regular church at all.

Even so, the bells in the church tower still toll at 6 a.m., noon and 6 p.m. every day to signal the time when residents can pray to the Angelus, a special prayer to Mary. And every morning the church itself is filled with those on hand for Mass.

"We may not be sending out as many priests and nuns any more, but that doesn't mean we've given up on our faith," said James Taylor, a longtime church member.

"We're still Catholics. We still believe. And we still work very, very hard for our church."

REDEMPTORISTS WHO HAVE COME FROM ST. ALPHONSUS, GRAND RAPIDS

The following short biographies of hometown sons of Saint Alphonsus and Grand Rapids who became Redemptorist priests and brothers testify to the tremendous contribution St. Alphonsus Parish has made to the building up of God's kingdom and the spiritual development of the Catholic Church throughout the world. In the history of Saint Alphonsus Parish, Grand Rapids, the laborers from the N.E. neighborhood in the Lord's vineyard have been remarkably many and the harvest has been plenty!

---

†REV. LIGUORI NUGENT
Ordained May 29, 1921

Born in Cannonsburg, MI, August 14, 1894; professed at Mount St. Clement College, DeSoto, MO, August 2, 1916; ordained at Immaculate Conception Seminary, Oconomowoc, WI, May 29, 1921. He was a large man with a booming missionary voice. He ministered principally on the West Coast and Midwest; his list of apostolic works totaled 303 missions, 263 retreats (45 to priests), 143 novenas and 184 shorter works. Spent last 24 years of his life at Glenview. He had a great devotion to the Blessed Sacrament and the Blessed Mother and always carried her rosary with him. He died with it in his hands at the age of 66 in 1960 at Villa Redeemer, Glenview, IL. 44 years professed, 39 years ordained.

†REV. FRANCIS DALTON
Ordained July 2, 1923

Born in Grand Rapids, MI, June 4, 1896; professed at DeSoto, MO, August 2, 1918; ordained at Immaculate Conception Seminary, Oconomowoc, WI, July 2, 1923. A missionary most of his life, he was said to have a voice that could be heard on the moon and beyond. He was stationed for a time in Portland, OR, and Whittier, CA. He had a remarkable memory seeming to be able to remember a page of print with one look. Despite poor eyesight, he remained as active as he could in his latter years. His genuine piety was an example to his confreres. Died suddenly at age 72 in 1968 while stationed at Holy Redeemer, Detroit, MI and on a visit to his sisters in Grand Rapids, MI. 50 years professed; 45 years ordained. Buried in Mt. Calvary Cemetery, Grand Rapids, MI along with his brother Rev. Richard Dalton.

†REV. BERNARD CONNELLY
Ordained July 2, 1923

Born in Penfield, PA, September 18, 1896; professed at Mount St. Clement College, DeSoto, MO, August 2, 1918; ordained at Immaculate Conception Seminary, Oconomowoc, WI, July 2, 1923. He served as a parish priest, rector, and missionary. A very capable teacher in the major seminary, his students bemoaned his toughness but had to admit he taught them to think. In fact, he was tough all his life and made difficult decisions without too much strain. He said, "he called 'em as he saw 'em." He was plagued with poor eyesight in his last years. Died at the age of 77 in 1974 at Immaculate Conception Health Care Center, Oconomowoc, WI. 55 years professed; 50 years ordained.

†REV. EDWARD JENNINGS
Ordained July 2, 1925

Born in Grand Rapids, MI, December 16, 1898; professed at Mount St. Clement College, DeSoto, MO, August 3, 1920; ordained at Immaculate Conception Seminary, Oconomowoc, WI, July 2, 1925. His long career began with teaching natural sciences in minor seminaries at St. Joseph College in Kirkwood, MO and at Holy Redeemer College in Oakland, CA after attending St. Louis University. While most of his life was spent on the West Coast as a missionary, he spent a few years working out of Villa Redeemer in Glenview, IL. He was the first retreat master at Redemptorist Palisades Retreat Center in Federal Way, WA, and served as Novice Master and as Director of the pastoral year program for young priests in the Oakland Province. He translated Bouchage's Pratique des vertus, which was used for morning meditation in many communities. He loved mission preaching and work with converts. He is always mentioned with loving respect by his confreres. Died at the age of 96 in 1995 at St. Clement Health Care Center, Liguori, MO. 75 years professed; 70 years ordained.

†REV. RICHARD DALTON
Ordained July 2, 1926

Born in Grand Rapids, MI, September 25, 1898; professed at Mount

St. Clement College, DeSoto, MO, August 2, 1921; ordained at Immaculate Conception Seminary, Oconomowoc, WI, July 2, 1926. He followed his brother, Francis, into the Redemptorists. He was a parish priest and missionary in many communities of the Midwest, and served as the Director of the Second Novitiate for two years. A simple, unassuming man, he suffered from Addison's disease for many years, although he continued to be active until his ill health forced him into retirement in 1969. He was the last confrere to die as a member of the St. Louis Province before the formation of the Denver Province. Died at the age of 97 in 1996 at St. Clement Health Care Center, Liguori, MO. 74 years professed; 69 years ordained.

†REV. DONALD F. MILLER
Ordained June 12, 1927

Born in Grand Rapids, MI, June 27, 1903; professed at Mount St. Clement College, DeSoto, MO, August 2, 1922; ordained at Immaculate Conception Seminary, Oconomowoc, WI, June 12, 1927. He was professor of Philosophy at the major seminary in Oconomowoc and Rector there (1942-1947).

Considered the founding Father of Liguori Publications. He edited the Liguorian for over 20 years in Oconomowoc and Liguori, MO. He published over 2,000 articles, pamphlets, and books during his life and collaborated with L.X. Aubin in writing the life of St. Alphonsus. After the amputation of a leg, he continued writing, lecturing, and making himself available to everyone. As one person said: "With his impressive devotion to truth, he was the epitome of the wise man who sees everything in perspective and gives all its proper weight." Died at the age of 66 in 1969 while stationed at St. Alphonsus "Rock" Parish, St. Louis, MO. 47 years professed; 42 years ordained.

†REV. RAYMOND J. MILLER
Ordained June 12, 1927

Born in Grand Rapids, MI, December 8, 1901; professed at Mount St. Clement College, DeSoto, MO, August 2, 1922; ordained at Immaculate Conception Seminary, Oconomowoc, June 12, 1927. He was a teacher at the minor seminary before receiving a doctorate in Canon Law from the Angelicum in Rome. He taught in the major seminary for 19 years, serving also as Prefect of Students for 14 years. He was Superior at St. John the Evangelist Parish in Carlisle, KY, at St. Alphonsus Parish in Davenport, IA, and at Villa Redeemer Retreat

Center in Glenview, IL, as well as a parish assistant and missionary. He served as a Consultor General in Rome (1958-1963). He lived a full life of service to the Church. He was a deeply spiritual man who was greatly revered. Died at the age of 86 in 1988 at Immaculate Conception Health Care Center, Oconomowoc, WI. 66 years professed; 61 years ordained.

†REV. ERNEST MILLER
Ordained June 29, 1931

Born in Grand Rapids, MI, January 25, 1905; professed at Mount St. Clement College, DeSoto, MO, August 2, 1926; ordained at Immaculate Conception Seminary, Oconomowoc, WI, June 29, 1931. He was one of the four Miller brothers who became Redemptorist priests from Grand Rapids in the St. Louis Province. He was a teacher in the minor seminary, parish missionary, military chaplain, and missionary in Thailand. He wrote many articles for the Liguorian. He directed more than 200 priests' retreats throughout the country. He was a pioneer at Liguori Publications. Died of a heart attack at the age of 72 in 1977 at Liguori Mission House, Liguori, MO. 50 years professed; 45 years ordained.

†REV. AUGUST PETERS
Ordained June 29, 1933

Born in Grand Rapids, December 29, 1906; professed at Mount St. Clement College, DeSoto, MO, August 2, 1928; ordained at Immaculate Conception Seminary, Oconomowoc, WI, June 29, 1933. He served two tours of duty in the Army and Air Force (1943-1947; 1948-1957) in many remote sections of the world. On his return from service, he served as a parish missionary and parish assistant. He was never one to sit still, and remained active until his death. Died at the age of 79 in 1986 at St. Alphonsus Parish, Grand Rapids, MI. 58 years professed; 53 years ordained.

†REV. MARK VAN GORP
Ordained June 29, 1934

Born in Grand Rapids, May 15, 1907; professed at Mount St. Clement College, DeSoto, MO; ordained at Immaculate Conception Seminary, Oconomowoc, WI, June 29, 1934. He was a parish priest and missionary and, in his later years, he assisted in diocesan parishes. During World War II, he served as a chaplain in the Army from 1942-1946. At the time of his death, he was serving as chaplain at St. Anne Retirement Home, Grand Rapids. He died at the age of 80 in 1987. 57 years professed; 53 years ordained.

†REV. ROBERT BOUCHER
Ordained June 28, 1935

Born in Grand Rapids, July 3, 1910; professed at Mount St. Clement College, DeSoto, MO, August 2, 1930; ordained at Immaculate Conception Seminary, Oconomowoc, WI, June 28, 1935. The first of three Boucher brothers to become Redemptorists. He resided at the Redemptorist Collegio Maggiore in Rome (1936-1939), while obtaining a Doctorate in Sacred Theology at the Gregorianum University and a Licentiate at the Biblical Institute summa cum laude. He taught Scripture for 27 years in the major seminary at Oconomowoc before he became a parish priest in 1966. Died suddenly at the age of 61 in 1971 at St. Alphonsus Parish, Grand Rapids, MI. 41 years professed; 36 years ordained.

†REV. FRANCIS TOBIN
Ordained June 29, 1938

Born in Grand Rapids, MI, August 11, 1912; professed at Mount St. Clement College, DeSoto, MO, August 2, 1933; ordained at Immaculate Conception Seminary, Oconomowoc, WI, June 29, 1938. With the outbreak of World War II, he enlisted in the U.S. Army as a chaplain and served in two theaters of war: the invasions at Salerno and the beach-head of Anzio, Italy. These were shattering emotional experiences for him, memories which never left him. He found himself more suited to taking the place of pastors than to a sustained assignment at one place, working from St. Alphonsus Parish, San Leandro, CA; the Center for Parish Missions, Oakland; and Sacred Heart Parish, Seattle, WA. He was deeply devoted to his large family and found relaxation in gardening. Died at the age of 79 in 1992 at the Center for Parish Missions, Oakland, CA. 58 years professed; 53 years ordained.

†REV. LOUIS BROWN
Ordained June 29, 1939

Born in Grand Rapids, January 6, 1913; professed at Mount St. Clement College, DeSoto, MO, August 2, 1934; ordained at Immaculate Conception Seminary, Oconomowoc, WI, June 29, 1939. He was a much loved parish priest all his active life. He was a man who was always available to the needs of the people of the parish as well as those of his confreres. He served for 17 years as minister at St. Michael Parish, Chicago, IL. Died at the age of 74 in 1987 at St. Alphonsus Parish, Grand Rapids, MI. 53 years professed; 48 years ordained.

†REV. LOUIS MILLER
Ordained June 29, 1939

Born in Grand Rapids, MI, April 11, 1913; professed at Mount St. Clement College, DeSoto, MO, August 2, 1934; ordained at Immaculate Conception Seminary, Oconomowoc, WI, June 29, 1939. The youngest of the four Miller brothers, he served as an Army chaplain in New Guinea during World War II, and later in Korea. Most of his active life he worked as a retreat preacher in great demand by priests and religious. He shared in the writing apostolate all his life by magazine articles and editorials, pamphlets, etc. He served as editor of the Liguorian Magazine (1961-1977). He also served at Mary, Mother of the Church Parish in South St. Louis County, MO and was Rector of the Ferguson, MO novitiate. Devoted to social justice issues, he served on the St. Louis Archdiocesan Commission on Human Rights, whose members remember him as "a steady and gentle defender of the dignity of all." To know him was to love him: saintly, humorous, unassuming, wise, interested in all. Died suddenly at the age of 81 in 1994 while stationed at Liguori Mission House, Liguori, MO. 60 years professed; 55 years ordained.

†REV. DONALD SCHUMAKER
Ordained June 29, 1940

Born in Burnips Corners, MI, August 12, 1913; professed at Mount St. Clement College, DeSoto, MO, August 2, 1935; ordained at Immaculate Conception Seminary, Oconomowoc, WI, June 29, 1940. He was a parish priest most of his life. He put his heart and soul into whatever work he was given. He had a saying: "life is short, let's enjoy it; the priesthood is important, let's work at it;" he did both. Died of a stroke at St. Mary Hospital, Kansas City at the age of 57 in 1970 while stationed at Our Lady of Perpetual Help, Kansas City, MO. 35 years professed; 30 years ordained.

†REV. THOMAS TOBIN
Ordained June 29, 1940

Born in Grand Rapids, MI, March 11, 1914; professed at Mount St. Clement College, DeSoto, MO, August 2, 1935; ordained at Immaculate Conception Seminary, Oconomowoc, WI, June 29, 1940. He was a Philosophy teacher at Oconomowoc. He pioneered at Liguori Mission House in Liguori, MO and later became Rector there. He began publication of the Scrupulous Anonymous Bulletin. He actively engaged in the apostolate to divorced Catholics and marriage counseling. He was Superior at Holy Redeemer College in Waterford, WI and Pastor at St. Brigid Parish in Midland, MI. He died suddenly at the age of 64 in 1978 at Holy Name Parish, Omaha, NE. 43 years professed; 38 years ordained.

†REV. GERARD BOUCHER
Ordained July 2, 1941

Born in Grand Rapids, MI, November 10, 1914; professed at Mount St. Clement College, DeSoto, MO, August 2, 1936; ordained at Immaculate Conception Seminary, Oconomowoc, July 2, 1941. Most of his active life was dedicated to preaching missions, from 1946 until shortly before his death. He was a fine preacher and retreat master. His two brothers, Robert and John, were also Redemptorists. Cancer cut short his productive life. He died at the age of 66 in 1981 at Perpetual Help Retreat House, Oconomowoc, WI. 45 years professed; 40 years ordained.

†FR. LEO DILLENBECK
Clerical Student for Priesthood
Professed August 2, 1941

Born in Grand Rapids, MI, June 21, 1920; professed at Mount St. Clement College, DeSoto, MO, August 2, 1941. He followed his brother, Frederick, into the Congregation. Died at the age of 21 in 1941 at Immaculate Conception Seminary, Oconomowoc, WI breaking through the ice while ice skating on Lake Lac La Belle while trying to save a fellow student, Frater William Doolan, who also perished. 5 months professed.

†REV. FREDERICK DILLENBECK
Ordained June 29, 1943

Born in Grand Rapids, MI, April 4, 1917; professed at Mount St. Clement College, DeSoto, MO, August 2, 1938; ordained at Immaculate Conception Seminary, Oconomowoc, WI, June 29, 1943. He served as parish priest during his short life. He died of leukemia at the age of 39 in 1956 at St. Mary Assumption, New Orleans, LA. 18 years professed; 13 years ordained.

†REV. BERNARD TOBIN
Ordained July 29, 1943

Born in Grand Rapids, MI, July 26, 1915; professed August 2, 1938; ordained at Immaculate Conception Seminary, Oconomowoc, WI, July 29, 1943. His brothers, Frank and Gerard, were also Redemptorists. In California, he served as Superior and Pastor at St. Alphonsus Parish, San Leandro; St. Alphonsus Parish, Fresno; and St. Jude Parish, Fresno. He died at at age of 69 in 1985 as the result of a beating during an armed robbery at St. Alphonsus' rectory in Fresno. 46 years professed; 42 years ordained.

†BRO. JAMES (MELBOURNE) BOHR
Professed October 16, 1943

Born in Grand Rapids, MI, June 3, 1919; professed at Mount St. Clement College, DeSoto, MO, October 16, 1943. He spent 34 years in the parish offices and sacristies of St. Joseph Parish in Wichita, KS, at Our Lady of Perpetual Help in Kansas City, MO and both St. Alphonsus and St. Michael Parishes in Chicago, as well as 13 years with the Co-Redemptorist Office. He wrote "I find [Redemptorist] life more agreeable than I first expected. I can truly say I am happier now than ever before." A gentle, considerate man, he was active in prayer groups and Bible studies; he was very devoted to the Mother of God. Died at age 70 in 1990 at St. Alphonsus Parish, Chicago, IL. 46 years professed.

†REV. GEORGE LIESVELD
Ordained January 6, 1949

Born in Grand Rapids, MI, October 18, 1922; professed at Mount St. Clement College, DeSoto, MO, August 2, 1943; ordained at Immaculate Conception Seminary, Oconomowoc, WI, January ;6, 1949. He served as Socius, counselor, and teacher of English and Latin at the minor seminaries at St. Joseph College in Kirkwood, MO and St. Joseph Preparatory College in Edgerton, WI. In 1969, when leaders were elected and not appointed, he was among the first elected to the Ordinary Provincial Council of the St. Louis Province. He was always gentle and generous in his many years as a parish priest. Died at the age of 69 in 1992 at St. Clement Health Care Center, Liguori, MO. 48 years professed; 43 years ordained.

†REV. EDWARD NUGENT
Ordained January 6, 1949

Born in Grand Rapids, MI, November 17, 1922; professed at Mount St. Clement College, DeSoto, MO, August 2, 1943; ordained at Immaculate Conception Seminary, Oconomowoc, WI, January 6, 1949. He was Rector at Perpetual Help Retreat Center, Oconomowoc and first Pastor and Superior at Mary, Mother of the Church Parish, South St. Louis Country, MO. He devoted most of his life to missions and retreats. His heart was open to everyone; he was "a good listener" to all who needed attention. He died suddenly at age 60 in 1983 at Villa Christi Retreat House,

Wichita, KS. 39 years professed; 34 years ordained.

†REV. GERARD TOBIN
Ordained June 29, 1949

Born in Grand Rapids, MI, November 24, 1922; professed at Mount St. Clement College, DeSoto, MO, August 2, 1944; ordained at Immaculate Conception Seminary, Oconomowoc, WI, June 29, 1949. Known as "Padre Rafael" among the Brazilian people to whom he had dedicated his life; he was also called "Padre Bondoso" (The Kind Priest). He died of a brain tumor at the age of 42 in 1965 at Holy Redeemer Seminary, Belem, Brazil. Buried in Grand Rapids. 20 years professed; 15 years ordained.

†REV. JAMES JOSEPH NUGENT
Ordained June 29, 1950

Born in Grand Rapids, MI, October 29, 1924; professed at Mount St. Clement College, DeSoto, MO, August 2, 1945; ordained at Immaculate Conception Seminary, Oconomowoc, WI, June 29, 1950. First assignment was as Socius (assistant novice master) at Desoto, MO. In 1953 he became the first full blooded Irishman to be stationed in the predominately German Redemptorist community at St. Michael's Church in Chicago, IL. Later he served as an assistant pastor at Our Lady of Perpetual Help Church in Kansas City, MO from 1958 to 1961; St. Alphonsus Parish in Davenport, IA from 1961-1964; and as Pastor of St. Joseph Parish in Denver, CO from 1964 to 1968. From 1969 to until 1978 he was associate pastor at St. Alphonsus Parish in Brooklyn Center, MN and from 1978 to 1980 at St. Joseph Parish in Wichita, KS. He was a retreat Master at Our Mother of Perpetual Help Retreat Center, Oconomowoc, WI for one year before returning to parish ministry at Holy Ghost Parish in Houston, TX between 1981 and 1984. From 1984 to 1986 he was Pastor and Superior of the community in St. Anthony Parish in Okmulgee, OK and from 1986 to 1996 as Pastor and superior of Holy Redeemer Parish in Odessa, TX. He achieved a great reputation through the years as an excellent parish priest and pastor. Died at St. Clement Health Care Center April 9, 2012 and is buried next to his two brothers at Liguori, MO. 66 years professed; 61 years ordained.

† REV. WILLIAM A. NUGENT
Ordained July 2, 1951

Born in Grand Rapids, MI, September 2, 1926; professed at Mount St. Clement College, DeSoto, MO, August 2, 1946; ordained at Immaculate Conception Seminary,

Oconomowoc, WI, July 2, 1951. He was the only St. Louis Provincial Superior to die in office. He followed his uncle and two brothers into the Congregation and served over 30 years in Brazil, where he was Vice-Provincial Vicar; administrator of the Prelacy of Coari; Superior and Pastor at Manaus, Belem, and Coari. A man of strong faith and deep love of the Church and Congregation, his Irish wit endeared him to all. He courageously endured cancer and died as Provincial of the St. Louis Province at the age of 63 in 1990 at the Province headquarters at Villa Redeemer, Glenview, IL. He is buried next to his brothers, Edward and James at Liguori, MO. 43 years professed; 38 years ordained.

†REV. JOHN BOUCHER
Ordained June 26, 1952

Born in Grand Rapids, MI, March 6, 1926; professed at Mount St. Clement College, DeSoto, MO, August 2, 1947; ordained at Immaculate Conception Seminary, Oconomowoc, WI, June 26, 1952. He was the youngest of three brothers who became Redemptorists. Going to Thailand in 1954, he found the first years quite difficult. A sensitive man, he had to deal with times of depression, but worked over 30 years in the Vice-Province, mainly in the Bangkok parish. In 1988, he returned to the U.S. and was stationed at Perpetual Help Retreat in Oconomowoc, and later for a short time at St. Alphonsus Parish in Brooklyn Center, MN before being appointed Director of the St. Louis Province Mission Office at Glenview in 1991. He died suddenly at the age of 70 in 1996 covering a preaching date in Grand Rapids while stationed at Villa Redeemer, Glenview, IL. Buried in Glenview. 49 years professed; 44 years ordained.

REV CHARLES BUECHE
Ordained June 29, 1953

Born in Grand Rapids, MI, April 27, 1927; professed at Mount St. Clement College, DeSoto MO, August 2, 1948; ordained at Immaculate Conception Seminary, Oconomowoc, WI, June 29, 1953. In February 1955 Father Chuck left for Bangkok, Thailand, studied the language and then was assigned in October to northeast Thailand. In 1957 he became Pastor of the biggest parish at that time in Udon. In 1961 he became pastor at Nongkhai. In 1968 he was asked to teach English to 30 Thai seminarians who would later study in English in the Seminary in Malaysia. He also was a chaplain to American Marine forces based in Thailand often going by jeep or helicopter escorted by Green Berets. In 1969 Father Chuck became Pastor of BiengKuhk. In the autumn of that year he returned to the United States, hoping for an assignment to the Alaskan missions, but was sent to St. Alphonsus Parish in Chicago. There he taught religion to the 500 children of the grade school, served as a chaplain to all the boy and girl scouts and was in charge of the 960 seat Anthenaem Theatre, which was used for various parish and public events. After further assignments between 1978 and 1985 in Denver and Wichita, Father Chuck began a long career in 1985 as a promoter for the Liguorian Magazine at Liguori, MO. He drove over 20,000 miles each year preaching in over 40 parishes a year in over 50 dioceses in support of the apostolate of the pen. By 1992 bad eyesight and other emerging infirmities limited his activity to soliciting Liguorian dates by phone and doing local help out work around St. Louis. He retired to St. Clement Health Care Center in 2006 where he currently resides and loves to make rosaries for the missions.

REV. JAMES RICHARD KEENA
Ordained July 2, 1957

Born in Grand Rapids, MI, April 10, 1931; professed at Mount St. Clement College, DeSoto, MO, August 2, 1952; ordained at Immaculate Conception Seminary, Oconomowoc, WI, July 2, 1957. After ordination Father Jim studied moral theology at the Alphonsian Academy in Rome. Upon returning to the United States he served as a missionary out of Holy Redeemer Church, Detroit, MI and served as a parish priest at Our Lady of Perpetual Help Church, Kansas City, MO. Father then did graduate studies in mathematics and began teaching math, algebra, geometry, and trigonometry at St. Joseph's Preparatory College in Edgerton, Wi from 1964 to 1972. He was then assigned to be the Dean of Men for Redemptorist Theology students at Esopus, NY where he served from 1972 to 1978. From 1978 Father Jim served six years as Pastor of St. Brigid's Parish, Midland MI, six year as Pastor of St. Gerard's Parish, Brooklyn Park, MN, and nine years as Pastor of St. Michael's Parish in Chicago until 1999. In July of 1999, he was elected provincial consultor and Vicar of the Denver Province, serving until 2002. He then became Pastor of Holy Name Parish, Omaha, NE from 2002 to 2005. Next Father Jim served as the local superior at Liguori Mission House at Liguori, MO. Since 2008 Father has served as a senior priest in residence at

Our Lady of Sorrows, Biloxi, MS and St. Michael's Church, Chicago where he currently resides.

†REV. BERNARD G. ROONEY
Ordained July 2, 1959

Born in Grand Rapids, July 8, 1933; professed at Mount St. Clement College, DeSoto, MO, August 2, 1954; ordained at Immaculate Conception Seminary, Oconomowoc, WI, July 2, 1959. "Turk," as he was known to his confreres, worked for many years as a parish priest, seminary teacher, and as the Director of the Co-Redemptorist Association. He received his Doctorate in Theology from the Angelicum in Rome, and he used his knowledge as professor at the major seminaries in Oconomowoc and Mount St. Alphonsus Seminary in Esopus, NY. Besides co-ordinating the Co-Redemptorist Association, he served as a parish priest at St. Michael Parish in Chicago, IL and Holy Redeemer Parish in Detroit, MI. He lived the last 23 years of his life at St. Alphonsus in Grand Rapids serving as parish priest, missionary preacher and parish administrator. He gave himself wholeheartedly to whatever he was called to do. Died at the age of 75 in 2008 at St. Alphonsus Parish, Grand Rapids, MI. 54 years professed, 49 years ordained.

REV. WILLIAM VERNON WRIGHT
Ordained June 29, 1960

Born in Grand Rapids, MI, December 28, 1933; professed at Mount St. Clement College, DeSoto, MO, August 2, 1955; ordained at Immaculate Conception Seminary, Oconomowoc, WI, June 29, 1960. Father Bill, originally interested in going to the Brazilian mission, ended up ministering in Thailand from 1963 to 2010. He was stationed at St. Alphonsus, Nongkhai, Thailand most of his years there as a base to go out into the interior of Thailand and minister to various Thai, Lao and Vietnamese populations. He often travelled by motor scooter in all sorts of weather conditions. He was also a confessor to Redemptorist novices in what was supposed to be a temporary appointment but lasted 12 years and was renewed for another 12 years! He returned to the United States in 2010 and presently ministers at his home parish of St. Alphonsus in Grand Rapids as a senior priest in residence, saying Masses, hearing confessions and assisting at area nursing homes.

BR. LEO EDWARD PATIN
Professed August 2, 1961

Born in Grand Rapids March 3, 1942; professed at Mount St. Clement College, DeSoto, MO,

August 2, 1961. The second of the five Patin Brothers to join the Redemptorists, Brother Leo, after his profession in 1961 first spent 11 years at St. Joseph's Preparatory College, the Redemptorist Seminary High School in Edgerton, Wisconsin. He was the chief engineer for the college's elaborate high pressure heating systems, its own water tower, water supply and sewage treatment plant. Next he was assigned to Perpetual Help Retreat Center at Oconomowoc, Wisconsin, spending 16 years overseeing the retreat center's facilities. He was then asked to join the newly established St. Clement Health Care Center at Liguori Missouri for Redemptorists needing nursing care and used his talents to oversee the maintenance of its facilities. In 1992, at the age of 50, Brother Leo went to the Redemptorist Brazilian missions and labored along the Amazon River. He was based in Coari, Amazonas, Brazil and it was there that he founded and administrated the St. Gerard's Youth Center and Trade School, teaching impoverished youth trade skills that would lead to employment and advancement. In 2009 he returned to the United States, where he briefly spent time in Oakland California. Presently Brother Leo serves as the Senior Redemptorist in residence at the student philosophy residence in the Bronx, N.Y. accompanying the students as a mentor.

†REV. ROBERT EARL
Ordained July 2, 1963

Born in Grand Rapids, MI, September 14, 1937; professed at Mount St. Clement College, DeSoto, MO, August 2, 1958; ordained at Immaculate Conception Seminary, Oconomowoc, WI, July 2, 1963. He was a professor of English at Holy Redeemer College, Waterford, WI, for 16 years. He served as Superior at Sacred Heart Retreat House, Rolling Meadows, IL. He was known as an activist for the underprivileged, homeless, and those living in substandard conditions and a congenial confrere to live with in community. He was diagnosed with cancer while stationed at St. Alphonsus "Rock" Parish, St. Louis, MO. Died at the age of 53 in 1991 at St. Clement Health Care Center, Liguori, MO. 32 years professed; 27 years ordained.

†REV. LAWRENCE PATIN
Ordained July 2, 1963

Born in Grand Rapids MI, October 1, 1937; professed at Mount St. Clement College, DeSoto, MO, August 2, 1958; ordained at Immaculate Conception Seminary,

Oconomowoc, WI, July 2, 1963. He was the first of five brothers to become Redemptorists. Father Larry ministered in the Vice Province of Bangkok (now the Province of Thailand) for 45 years. He was Pastor at Khon Kaen, Nongkhai and Pattaya. He taught at the minor seminary at Sriracha, and was Novice Master at Nongkhai. He served two terms on the Extraordinary Vice Provincial Council and on the Ordinary Vice Provincial Council as Vicar. He last served as Director of the Redemptorist Center in Pattaya and Director of the Father Ray Brennan Foundation. He is fondly remembered throughout Thailand for his great energy, leadership skills, and especially his heartfelt dedication to the poor and needy, as well as to the children and youth. He was diagnosed with a brain tumor and returned to the United States where he died at Saint Clement Health Care Center at Liguori, MO at the age of 73 in 2011. Buried in the family plot in Sand Lake, MI. 52 years professed, 47 years ordained.

BR. ANDREW MICHAEL PATIN
Professed August 2, 1964

Born in Grand Rapids, MI, August 15, 1943; professed at Mount St. Clement College, Desoto, MO, August 2, 1964. Brother Andy, after a year at Oconomowoc WI, went to Holy Name Parish, Omaha NE from1965 to 1967, after which he went to St. Joseph's Preparatory College for a year before going to second novitiate in preparation for final vows in 1968. After final vows he was stationed in Oconomowoc and Villa Redeemer, Glenview, IL. In 1971 Brother Andy received his first appointment to his home parish, St. Alphonsus. Grand Rapids, MI. After seven years he had appointments to Villa Redeemer, Glenview and Holy Redeemer College, Waterford WI. He then went to St. Alphonsus, Chicago IL where he spent the next 14 years in parish ministry and sacristy/office service. Brother Andy returned to his home parish in 2000 where he currently serves and has distinguished himself in ministry to the sick and shut-ins of the parish.

†BRO. PAUL RICHARD (RAYMOND) BOWERSOX
Professed August 2, 1965

Born in Grand Rapids, MI August 18, 1928; professed at Mount St. Clement College, DeSoto, MO, August 2, 1965. Br. Raymond served in the U.S. Army in the 1950s and later began a career with the U.S. Post Office. He felt the call to religious life and in 1965 professed vows as a Redemptorist and "Raymond" as his religious name. Br. Raymond served briefly at Our Mother of Perpetual Help Retreat Center in Oconomowoc, WI and St. Michael Parish in Chicago, but is best remembered for his time at Holy Redeemer College in Waterford, WI from 1970 to 1978. He is remembered especially for his patience in taking care of an elderly wheelchair bound priest well known for being demanding. He enjoyed spending time with seminarians, cheering on their sports teams, and often served as their chaperone to sporting events. Students loved him and kidded him by mimicking his stuttered speech and playing little tricks on him. Br. Raymond was appointed sacristan at St. Alphonsus Parish in Minneapolis, MN in 1987 — a position he held until his retirement in 2000. Ill health necessitated his move to St. Clement Health Care Center. Despite the tremendous physical pain that he endured, he remained a kind, cheerful and prayerful confrere. He died at the age of 84 in 2011 at St. Clement Health Care Center, Liguori, MO. 46 years professed.

BRO. EUGENE GREGORY PATIN
Professed August 2, 1965

Born in Grand Rapids, MI, March 30, 1946; professed at Mount St. Clement College, DeSoto, MO, August 2, 1965. His first assignments were to the Redemptorist seminaries in Wisconsin to maintain and operate the seminaries' Hvac systems. After 18 years Brother Gene began doing parish ministry, specifically to the poor and marginalized at Blessed Sacrament Parish in Southside inner city Chicago, Holy Name Parish in inner city Memphis, TN, Mother of Sorrows Parish in Biloxi, Mississippi and St. Gerard's Parish in Baton Rouge, LA, where he currently serves. Many of his efforts are aimed at economic advancement and opportunities for youth. He also served on the Denver Province extraordinary council from 2002 to 2005.

†FR. JOSEPH ANDRE
Clerical Student for Priesthood
Professed August 2, 1966

Born in Grand Rapids, MI, March 10, 1945; professed at Mount St. Clement College, DeSoto, MO. He died in 1968 at the age of 23 at Immaculate Conception Seminary, Oconomowoc, WI in an automobile accident near Oconomowoc, WI while returning from catechetical work among Spanish-speaking migrant workers. Buried from St. Alphonsus Church, Grand Rapids. His parents, Carl and Nellie, lived directly across the street from Saint Alphonsus. 2 years professed.

REV. HARRY ARTHUR GRILE
Ordained June 27, 1968

Born in Grand Rapids, MI, October 4, 1942; professed at Mount St. Clement College, DeSoto MO; August 2, 1963; ordained at Immaculate Conception Seminary, Oconomowoc, WI, June 27, 1968. The older of two brothers who became Redemptorists and cousins to the Redemptorist Nugent brothers, Father Harry began studies in 1970 in European history and then served as professor of Church history, vice president and academic dean at Mount St. Alphonsus Seminary in Esopus, NY from 1971 to 1984. From 1984 to 1986 he served as a missionary preacher out of St. Alphonsus Parish, Chicago. He then went to St. Alphonsus Parish in Brooklyn Center, MN as a parish priest and became its Pastor from 1987 to 1993. From there he was called to serve as Superior and Formation Director for the theology students from 1993 to 1999 at Blessed Sacrament Parish in Chicago and over saw the move to the Seelos House residence near the campus of Catholic Theological Union. From 1999 to 2006 he was President/Publisher of Liguori Publications. In 2007 he was named Pastor of Sacred Heart Parish in Seattle, WA. In 2011 Father Harry was elected and currently serves as Provincial Superior of the Denver Province.

BR. GERARD JOSEPH PATIN
Professed August 2, 1968

Born in Grand Rapids, MI, July 24, 1949; professed at Blessed John Neumann College (St. Iraneus, Church) Clinton, IA, August 2, 1968. His early years as a Redemptorist found him ministering in seminary formation and maintenance at St. Joseph's Preparatory College in Edgerton, Wisconsin. After many years in that position he went to Holy Redeemer Church in Detroit, Michigan where he was involved in parish ministry—especially with youth ministry He also became active in 12 step recovery programs. Next he was assigned to Perpetual Help Retreat Center in Oconomowoc, Wisconsin. After many years of maintaining the facilities there he was appointed Director of the Retreat Center where he presently serves. He is also presently serving as a member of the Denver Province Extraordinary Provincial Council.

REV. PATRICK JOSEPH GRILE
Ordained June 24, 1971

Born in Grand Rapids, MI, April 17, 1945; professed at Mount St. Clement College, DeSoto, MO,

August 2, 1966; ordained at Holy Redeemer College, Waterford, WI, June 24, 1971. Served as associate pastor at St. Alphonsus Chicago and St. Alphonsus, Broolyn Center, MN between 1972 and 1981. In 1981 Father Pat was assigned as Pastor of St. Gerard Majella Parish in Kirkwood, MO and under saw the completion of a new church and renovation of the old church into a multi-purpose building. In August of 1987 he was assigned as associate pastor at St. Joseph's Church, Wichita, KS and in 1989 as a high school and young adult retreat Master at Sacred Heart Retreat Center in Rolling Meadow, IL. In 1989 Father Pat "came home" as an associate pastor here at St. Alphonsus, Grand Rapids, MI for 10 years before being named Pastor of St. Alphonsus Parish, Brooklyn Center, MN. He was Pastor there for 12 years before coming "home" again in 2011 and presently serves as Pastor and Superior of the St. Alphonsus community in this Jubilee Year.

REV. WILLIAM CHARLES BUECHE
Ordained June 1, 1978

Born in Grand Rapids, MI, June 22, 1952; professed at Immaculate Conception Novitiate, Oconomowoc WI, August 5, 1973; ordained at Holy Redeemer College, Waterford, WI, June 1, 1978. Father Bill served as parochial vicar of Holy Name Church in Omaha, Nebraska before being assigned to Rome in 1980 to study moral theology earning a licentiate and a doctorate, subsequently staying in Rome to teach at the Alphonsian Academy from 1986 to 1996. Returned to the United States in 1996 and was pastor of Blessed Sacrament Parish until 2005 in inner city Chicago, which served both African Americans and Hispanics. He served on the Denver Province Extraordinary Provincial Council from 1999 to 2002. Since 2005, Father Bill currently serves in parish ministry at St. Alphonsus Parish in Minneapolis, MN working primarily with the Latino community.

REV. THOMAS MICHAEL SANTA
Ordained June 1, 1978

Born in Grand Rapids, MI, November 4, 1952; professed at Immaculate Conception Novitiate, Oconomowoc, WI, August 5, 1973; ordained at Holy Redeemer College, Waterford, WI, June 1, 1978. Father Tom was first assigned as a high school instructor at the Redemptorist minor seminaries first at St. Joseph's Preparatory College in Edgerton WI and later at St. Henry's Seminary in Belleville, IL. He was assigned to retreat ministry at Villa Christi Retreat Center, Wichita KS in 1983. During his time there he was instrumental in working with the Bishop of Wichita in building a new Spiritual Life Center complex and became its First Director. In 1992 he became President and Publisher of Liguori Publications and undertook a major expansion of its services. In 1997 he was named Director of the Picture Rocks Redemptorist Renewal Center in Tucson, AZ. He over saw major construction and upgrading of the retreat facilities and grounds and introduced many new retreat programs and concepts during his tenure. In 2011 he was named Pastor of St. Michael's Church in Old Town, Chicago IL where he presently serves.

REV. GARY EDWARD ZIURAITIS
Ordained June 1, 1978

Born in Grand Rapids, MI, June 4, 1949; professed at Holy Redeemer College, Waterford, WI, August 22, 1975; ordained at Holy Redeemer College, Waterford, WI, June 1, 1978. Father Gary served as associate pastor from 1979 to 1983 at the Redemptorist parishes of Mary, Mother of the Church in St. Louis, MO, St. Michael's in Chicago and St. Joseph's in Wichita, KS consecutively. From 1983 to 1992 he served at Liguori Publications as an assistant editor, columnist and promoter for the Liguorian, creator of parish education resources and Director of the A/V department, which won many awards for its sacramental and religious education videos; In 1992 he was appointed Pastor of St. William Parish and two missions in Fort Lupton, CO, which led to the study of the Spanish language to serve their Latino populations. In 1997, named Project Director and served as Executive Producer of the Redemptorist Hispanic Radio Project Tu Companero Catolico, which continued until 2011; served on the Denver Province Extraordinary Provincial Council from 1999 to 2002. Father Gary was named Director of Communications for the Redemptorist General Government, Rome, Italy in 2004 where he over saw communications between the 5,000 Redemptorists around the world and its General Government and served as an information officer to the public. He returned to the United States in 2013 and is currently serving in parish ministry at St. Gerard Parish in San Antonio, TX.

FR. AARON LEE MESZAROS
Clerical Student for Priesthood
Professed August 1, 2010

Born in Grand Rapids, MI June 22, 1985. Entered the Redemptorist formation program in 2007 and professed vows on August 1, 2010 at St. Alphonsus Church, Grand Rapids, MI while attending Catholic Theological Union in Chicagoand while residing at the Redemptorist student residence called Seelos House. Frater Aaron has one more year of theological studies and is currently participating in a pastoral immersion year in Redemptorist community and ministerial life at Holy Ghost Parish in Houston, TX in preparation for ordination.

The following spent time as professed students/brothers or ordained Redemptorists before discerning that God was calling them to another way of life:

James Bek
Richard Bek
Robert Bek
Thomas Brooks
Joseph Earl
Patrick Earl
Thomas Eggleston
Joseph Fron
Michael Hillary
Robert Hillary
Thomas Hillary
Richard Miller
Peter Patin
Steve Robach

Patrick Norton
John Otterbacher
Raymond Palmiter
Clemence Schwartz
†Terry Smith *(Stricken with cancer in the final months of novitiate in 1968. Chose not to be professed but returned home to Grand Rapids for treatment. He died January 1, 1970. Buried from St. Alphonsus.)*
Donald Symanski
James Thiel
Ron Ziuraitis

In addition, between 100 and 150 other young men from Grand Rapids and St. Alphonsus entertained the possibility of a call to the Redemptorist priesthood or brotherhood by attending the Redemptorist high school and college programs during their adolescent and formative years. After leaving the Redemptorist formation programs they went on to build up the Kingdom of God in service to their communities by their various chosen professions and many in service to God as husbands and fathers. Some are still numbered among the parishioners of Saint Alphonsus.

SONS OF ST. ALPHONSUS WHO BECAME DIOCESAN PRIESTS
(The Ones that Got Away!)

†Rev. Edmund Corby, Diocese of Grand Rapids
Rev. Joseph J. Fix, Diocese of Grand Rapids
†Rev. Joseph Grill, Diocese of Grand Rapids
Rev. Robert Miller, Archdiocese of Chicago
Rev. Thomas Page, Diocese of Grand Rapids
Tim Weed, preparing for ordination for the Congregation of the Holy Cross

CHAPTER 12
THE FERTILE FIELD OF VOCATIONS

The Harvest has always been plenty here with so many answering the call to serve in Religious life. In addition to the rich history of the Redemptorists who have come from our neighborhood we have been blessed with countless others who have answered God's call. Our rich tradition would not be what it is today if those courageous and brave Dominican Sisters hadn't been willing to come here to begin St. Johns Orphanage. That orphanage was really not in their "line of work"; they were established as a teaching order. However, their willingness to come to Grand Rapids delivered them right up the hill from the little school and parish that was being built simultaneously with St. Johns. One has to be convinced that God's hand was there as students and parishioners were taught and nurtured by these lovely women. Their courage and example help to yield a huge harvest.

Enjoy looking at the lists of all of the Religious vocations that have come from our neighborhood. Read with delight the story of the Miller family who produced

Captain Comer, CSsR, Army Chaplain

Fr. Ed Comer

109

five vocations, four Redemptorist Priests and a Redemptoristine Nun! Enjoy reading about the proud military careers of our Priests who not only served us but our country as well. And finally, for the first time you will be able to look at all 30 Pastors who wrote their legacy's on our hearts. They led with courage and conviction. Three of them came back to St. Al's twice to serve. And our dear Fr. Quinn, who loved us enough to go for a triple! Our debt of gratitude can never be expressed enough for their willingness to lead.

REDEMPTORIST MILITARY CHAPLAINS

Members of the St. Alphonsus Parish community have a long record of military service. Redemptorists associated with the parish have exercised their missionary spirit by serving as military chaplains during World War I, World War II, the Korean War, Vietnam War and Gulf War eras.

Fr. Quinn saying Mass for the troops

Rev. John Britz was an Army auxiliary chaplain in Oregon during World War I.

Rev. Ernest Miller served as an Army chaplain during World War II.

Rev. August Peters served as a chaplain during two tours of duty in the Army (1943-1947) and Air Force (1948-1957) in many remote sections of the world.

Rev. Mark Van Gorp served as chaplain in the Army during World War II from 1942-1946.

Rev. Edward Comer served for four years (1942-1946) as a military chaplain in the Army during the invasions of France and Germany in World War II.

Rev. Francis Tobin enlisted in the Army as a chaplain at the outbreak of World War II. He served from 1943-1946 in two theaters of war:

the invasions of Salerno and the beach-head of Anzio, Italy.

Rev. Louis Miller served as an Army chaplain in New Guinea during World War II and later in Korea.

Fr. Quinn distributing Communion to a soldier

Rev. Raymond Palmiter served during the 1960s as an Army chaplain in Germany.

Rev. Thomas Cosgrove served as an Air Force chaplain for five years (1954-1959); he was stationed in Okinawa and at the Vance Air Force Base in Enid, OK.

Rev. Edward Monroe served as an Auxiliary Chaplain in Thailand.

Rev. Richard Quinn served as an Army Chaplain for over six years (1988-1994) during the Gulf War Era. His brother Frank had served as a Marine in Vietnam and, after 25 years in parish service, Rev. Quinn realized his long-standing dream of serving as a military chaplain.

He gave the following interview to The Catholic Key—Newspaper of the Diocese of Kansas City /St. Joseph in 2012: "Catholic priests were in short supply in the military," Rev. Quinn said, so he volunteered. His application was accepted one week before he would have passed the age limit. He was 49 years old.

"I was told that if I volunteered for a 3-year tour, I would be turned down, but they'd accept me if I volunteered for five years. I said 'OK,' and made it 6 ½ years."

Rev. Quinn's military service spanned the years 1988-94, including the First Gulf War in 1990-91. He served a tour of duty at Fort Carson, near Colorado Springs, a tour at the US Army Garrison in Mannheim, Germany, and ended his volunteer military service at Fort Polk, near Leesville, Vernon Parish, La.

111

"I was in the army longer than I was in the minor seminary," he recalled with a grin. "Six and a half happy years, just the right amount of service."

He didn't spend all his time in Mannheim in the garrison. He made a military pilgrimage to Lourdes, "with 27,000 other soldiers." He toured St. Petersburg (Leningrad) and Moscow in a spirit of peace and reconciliation and was impressed by the sight of Germans and Russians "getting along." He traveled to Spain and to Strasbourg, France; visited the famous German spa at Baden-Baden, "but not the casinos;" he visited Rome, Dublin and Belfast and, as part of his professional development, toured significant World War II battlegrounds.

One of the reasons he volunteered for service as a military chaplain is what he calls the "underlying charism" of the Redemptorist community: to boldly defend the rights of Christ and His people. "We will fight," he said, "for the rights of the immigrant, the poor, the weak — Christ's people everywhere."

SR. MARY MARGARET MILLER O.SS.R.

Mary Margaret Miller was born on January 14, 1908 to Wenzel and Margaret (Hyland) Miller. Wenzel and Margaret had been married in 1899 and had a little home on Front St. that flooded periodically. The little family moved to St. Al's Parish and so the Miller story began. The Millers were first blessed with Raymond, Donald and Ernest before Mary Margaret came along. Another son followed Mary.

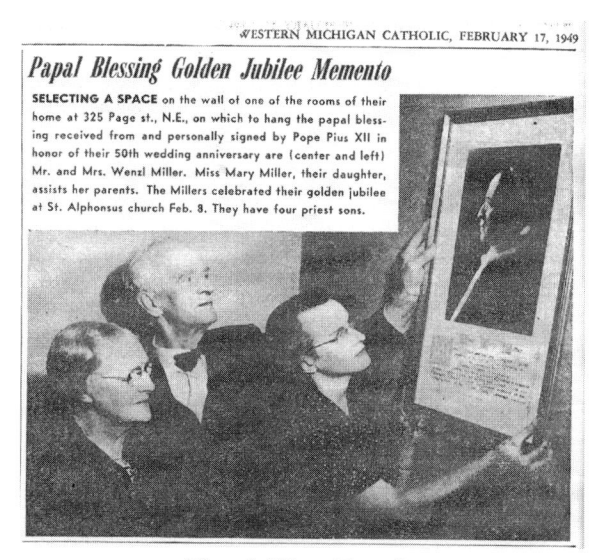

The Miller Family

Fast forward to one by one the oldest sons leave for the Redemptorist seminary. Margaret, being a good Catholic mother, was pleased that her sons were going into the Lord's service however difficult it was for her to send them off. Mary went about her education ending up at Marywood for high school. She wanted to continue her education at Aquinas College however the Great Depression hit and she had to go find a job. Meanwhile her youngest brother Louis was also desiring to attend the seminary as his brothers had. Margaret did not want to let another son go so he has the distinction of being the only Miller son to attend high school in Grand Rapids. After high school though he left for the Redemptorist formation program.

Mary Margaret worked for the Michigan Trust Bank for 20 years and took care of her parents. Her mother Margaret died suddenly in 1950 and then her Father, Wenzel in 1953. This allowed Mary the opportunity to answer the longing she had in her heart for religious life. Her spiritual director, a Dominican priest, Fr. Wilson exclaimed that "he was not surprised at all when she announced that she wished to become a Redemptoristine Nun"! However, none existed in the United States, with the closest group being in Canada in 1954. She was accepted and traveled to Canada to begin as a Postulant at the age of 45!

In 1960 Sr. Mary Margaret was sent to Ligouri, Missouri to begin a foundation of the order in the St. Louis Province. She served there until her death on March 19, 2010 at 102 years of age.

THE JOURNEY OF THE DOMINICAN SISTERS TO ST. ALPHONSUS

The journey of the Dominican Order in the United States began in 1853 when four cloistered Dominican nuns left Regensburg, Bavaria to go to New York to minister to German immigrants. These four brave women settled in Brooklyn in response to the call for religious teachers. In

October of 1877 the group in New York answered another request to come to Traverse City Michigan to open a school in a small wood framed home. The initial enrollment was six students but within two months that number grew to 50! Some of those students would be Michigans first candidates to the Dominican order.

With the building of St. Johns orphanage Bishop Richter requested that the Dominican sisters come to Grand Rapids as a new apostolate. "It was not an easy decision for Mother Aquinata's little band, which until then had regarded their mission as teaching. After prayerful discussion, however, they responded whole-heartedly to the obvious needs, and in May of 1888 Mother Aquinata and several Sisters arrived at the yet incomplete orphanage."

The early days for the Sisters were very difficult. The Sisters found it necessary to solicit provisions for the increasing number of children who came under their care. It was not uncommon to see one of the Sisters driving along the countryside in wooden cart with a kindly farmer assisting her as she went from door to door to collect produce for their home.

According to the Parish Annals of Sept. 2, 1889:

St. Alphonsus Parish School opened with four Dominican Sisters in charge. The pioneering sisters were: Sr. Cyprian, Sr. Sabina, Sr. Ignatius and Sr. Alacoque. There were 180 pupils enrolled at the opening of the school. The first student to graduate was Laetitia Traverse.

Dominican Sisters visiting St. Al's

For 125 years there were Dominican Sisters in our school with the final one being Sr. Olga Mizzi. We have been truly blessed with their love and dedication to the generations of children (and parents) that they education.

Thank you Sisters!!

RELIGIOUS VOCATIONS FROM ST. ALPHONSUS

REDEMPTORIST PRIESTS — ORDAINED

Rev. Liguori Nugent	May 29, 1921	*Uncle of Edward, James, & William*
Rev. Francis "Frank" Dalton	July 2, 1923	*Brother of Richard*
Rev. Bernard Connelly	July 2, 1923	
Rev. Edward Jennings	July 2, 1925	
Rev. Richard Dalton	July 2, 1926	*Brother of Frank*
Rev. Donald F. Miller	June 12, 1927	*Brother of Raymond, Ernest, & Louis*
Rev. Raymond J. Miller	June 12, 1927	*Brother of Donald, Ernest, & Louis*
Rev. Ernest Miller	June 29, 1931	*Brother of Donald, Raymond, & Louis*
Rev. August Peters	June 29, 1933	
Rev. Mark E. VanGorp	June 29, 1934	
Rev. Robert G. Boucher	June 28, 1938	*Brother of Gerard & John*
Rev. Francis "Frank" Tobin	June 29, 1938	*Brother of Bernard & Gerard*
Rev. Louis Brown	June 29, 1939	
Rev. Louis Miller	June 29, 1939	*Brother of Donald, Raymond, & Ernest*
Rev. Donald Schumaker	June 29, 1940	
Rev. Thomas Tobin	June 29, 1940	
Rev. Gerard Boucher	July 2, 1941	*Brother of Robert & John*
Rev. Frederick Dillenbeck	June 29, 1943	*Brother of Fr. Leo*
Rev. Raymond Palmiter	June 29, 1943	
Rev. Bernard Tobin	July 29, 1943	*Brother of Frank & Gerard*
Rev. Cyril Schmidt	January 6, 1949	
Rev. Robert Dillenbeck	January 6, 1949	
Rev. George Liesveld	January 6, 1949	
Rev. Edward Nugent	January 6, 1949	
Rev. Gerard Tobin	June 29, 1949	*Brother of Frank & Bernard*
Rev. James Joseph Nugent	June 29, 1950	*Brother of Edward & William*
V. Rev. William A. Nugent	July 2, 1951	*Brother of Edward & James*
Rev. John "Jack" Boucher	June 26, 1952	*Brother of Robert & Gerard*
Rev. Charles Bueche	June 29, 1953	
Rev. James Richard Keena	July 2, 1957	
Rev. Bernard G. "Turk" Rooney	July 2, 1959	

Rev. William Vernon Wright	June 29, 1960	
Rev. Joseph Earl	1961	
Rev. Robert Earl	July 2, 1963	
Rev. Michael James Hillary	July 2, 1963	
Rev. Lawrence Patin	July 2, 1963	*Brother of Leo, Andy, Eugene, & Gerard*
Rev. Robert Bek	July 2, 1963	
Rev. Joseph J. Fix	June 1, 1968	
Rev. Harry Arthur Grile	June 27, 1968	*Brother of Patrick*
Rev. Thomas Brooks	June 24, 1971	
Rev. James Thiel	June 24, 1971	
Rev. Patrick Joseph Grile	June 24, 1971	*Brother of Harry*
Rev. Robert Miller	June 3, 1976	
Rev. William Charles Bueche	June 1, 1978	
Rev. Thomas Michael Santa	June 1, 1978	
Rev. Gary Edward Ziuraitis	June 1, 1978	
Fra. Aaron Meszaros	Professed August 1, 2010	

DIED BEFORE ORDINATION — PROFESSED

Fra. Leo Dillenbeck	August 2, 1941
Fra. Joseph Andre	August 2, 1966

REDEMPTORIST BROTHERS — PROFESSED

Bro. Frank (Killian) Burns		
Bro. James (Melbourne) Bohr	October 16, 1943	
Bro. Leo Edward Patin	August 2, 1961	*Brother of Lawrence, Andy, Eugene, & Gerard*
Bro. Andrew Michael (Andy) Patin	August 2, 1964	*Brother of Lawrence, Leo, Eugene, & Gerard*
Bro. Paul Richard (Raymond) Bowersox	August 2, 1965	
Bro. Eugene Gregory Patin	August 2, 1965	*Brother of Lawrence, Leo, Andy, & Gerard*
Bro. Gerard Joseph Patin	August 2, 1968	*Brother of Lawrence, Leo, Andy, & Eugene*

DIOCESAN PRIESTS | ORDAINED

Rev. Edmund Corby — 1933
Rev. Walter Grill — 1938
Rev. Joseph Grill
Rev. James Fix
Rev. Thomas Page

HOLY CROSS BROTHERS

Bro. Richard Hesse

Fr. Denis Ryan's installation

Fr. Maurice Nutt preaching at the Parish Mission

Fr. Aaron Meszaros

Fr. Bill Bueche and Mr. May

Fr. Denis   Fr. Andy   Br. Andy   Fr. Bernie   Fr. Ed
Redemptorist Community 2009

Fr. Tony Judge at the Mission in February 2014

REDEMPTORISTINE SISTERS

Sr. Mary Margaret Miller, O.Ss.R. — 1956 *Sister of the 4 Miller brothers (Donald, Raymond, Ernest, & Louis) all of whom became Redemptorist priests*

DOMINICANS SISTERS — RELIGIOUS NAME

Lillian Finn	Sr. Mary Loyola, O.P.
Mary Finn	Sr. Mary Terencia, O.P.
Mary Walsh	Sr. Mary Dominica, O.P.
Louise Cornelissens	Sr. Mary Apollonia, O.P.
Sadie Impens	Sr. Mary Magdalen, O.P.
Catherine Pantus	Sr. Mary Zita, O.P.
Eleanore Murray	Sr. Mary Bernarda, O.P.
Ruth Patterson	Sr. Mary Georgiana, O.P.
Elizabeth Murphy	Sr. Mary Flavian, O.P.
Emma Forcht	Sr. Mary Nicholas, O.P.
Mary Bayer	Sr. Mary Felicia, O.P.
Alice Grypma	Sr. Mary Adorine, O.P.
Mary Mulvey	Sr. Edward Marie, O.P.
Hazel Visner	Sr. Mary Joachim, O.P.
Bernadine Visner	Sr. Perpetual Maria, O.P.
Cecil Visner	Sr. Elizabeth Mary, O.P.
Marie Visner	Sr. Rose Miriam, O.P.
Mary Boucher	Sr. Mary Leone, O.P.
Regina DeHaus	Sr. Rose Imelde, O.P.
Beatrice Ghering	Sr. Mary Virgil, O.P.
Agnes Bowkus	Sr. Mary Camilla, O.P.
Helen Palmetier	Sr. Mary Irenaea, O.P.
Mary DeHaus	Sr. Mary Liguori, O.P.
Helen Buech	Sr. Agnes Mary, O.P.
Anne Hamilton	Sr. Anne Jean, O.P.
Pauline Rode	Sr. Mary Barbara, O.P.
Eileen Bockheim	Sr. Mary Carletta, O.P.
Lillian Bockheim	Sr. Mary Gerarda, O.P.
Margaret Cronin	Sr. Mary Eunice, O.P.
Margaret Schneidr	Sr. Mary Peter, O.P.
Kay Rohloff	Sr. Ruth Mary, O.P.
Mary Ellen Novakowski	Sr. Matthew Mary, O.P.
Charline Heitz	Sr. Janet Marie, O.P.

Mary Ellen Barkwell	Sr. Mary Joellen, O.P.
Patricia Bowler	Sr. Mary Killian, O.P.
Ethel Shindorf	Sr. Mary Laverne, O.P.
Roberta Hefferan	Sr. Mary Thoma, O.P.

CONSOLATA SISTERS

Jo Williams	Sr. Jo Marie Williams, SM

LITTLE SISTERS OF THE POOR

Senna Grypma	Sr. Melaine de Alexis, PSDP

SISTERS OF MERCY

Eileen Tobin	Sr. Mary Lorraine, RSM
Magdalen Tobin	Sr. Mary Eileen, RSM
Ann Pantus	Sr. Mary Ann, RSM
Margaret Tolhurst	Sr. Mary Cyrilla, RSM
Corinne Bart	Sr. Mary Alphonse, RSM
Mary Heemstra	Sr. Ann Clare, RSM

SISTERS OF THE HOLY CROSS

Mary Doyle	Sr. Mary Edward, OSC
Madeline Holmes	Sr. Mary Violette, OSC
Eleanor Downs	Sr. Mary Harriet, OSC

SISTERS OF ST JOSEPH

Anastasia Connelly	Sr. Mary Emerentia, CSJ

SISTERS OF THE GOOD SHEPHERD

Irene Shilliday	Sr. Mary Aloysius, RGS
Dolores Hopper	Sr. Perpetual Help, RGS

FRANCISCAN SISTERS

Margaret DeHaus   Sr. Mary Audrey, OSF

SISTERS OF CHARITY

Josephine Moriarity *   Sr. Mary Cyprian, BVM
Margaret Glass   Sr. Mary Claudette, BVM

CARMELITE SISTERS

Mary Ann Siegal   Sr. Ann Therese, O. Carm
Joyce Kob   Sr. Margaret Mary, O. Carm
Susanne Ronan   Sr. Mary Susanne, O. Carm

MARYKNOLL SISTERS

Frances Kersjes   Sr. Mary Leo Anne, Maryknoll
Rosemary Tobin   Sr. Mary Rose Anne, Maryknoll

LADIES OF THE HEART OF MARY

Eva Visner

First girl from St Alphonsus Parish to enter a religious community.

ST. ALPHONSUS PASTORS

For the very first time, here are all of the wonderful men who have served our Parish as Pastors. Some were here for one assignment, three were assigned twice and one, Fr. Richard Quinn, blessed us with three assignments with us. We are truly blessed with their willingness to serve!

1888-1892
Fr. Theodore Lamy CSsR

1892-1893
Fr. Terence Clark CSsR

1893-1894
Fr. Ferreol Girardey CSsR

1894-1894
Fr. Daniel Mullane CSsR

1898-1901
Fr. Patrick Henry Barrett CSsR

1894-1898, 1901-1904
Fr. Joseph Distler CSsR

1904-1907
Fr. George Hild CSsR

1907-1909
Fr. Joseph Firle CSsR

1909-1912
Fr. Joseph Chapoton CSsR

1912-1918, 1939-1945
Fr. Edward Cantwell CSsR

1918-1921
Fr. Mathias Meyer CSsR

1921-1924
Fr. Patrick Dunne CSsR

1924-1927, 1955-1961
Fr. John Britz CSsR

1927-1930
Fr. Charles J Harrison CSsR

1930-1933
Fr. Thomas Condon CSsR

1933-1934
Fr. Marcellus Ryan CSsR

1934-1934
Fr. Walter L Polk CSsR

1945-1950
Fr. John F Daly CSsR

1950-1955
Fr. George Strass CSsR

1961-1967
Fr. Edmund Langton CSsR

1967-1971
Fr. Francis Novak CSsR

1971-1975, 1982-1987
Fr. Richard Quinn CSsR

1975-1977
Fr. Edward Monroe CSsR

1977-1981
Fr. Michael Hillar CSsR

1987-1993
Fr. Jack Dowd CSsR

1993-1999
Fr. Daniel Lowery CSsR

1999-2004
Fr. Tom Donaldson CSsR

2005-2007
Fr. Richard Quinn CSsR

2007-2011
Fr. Denis Ryan CSsR

2011-
Fr. Patrick Grile CSsR

CHAPTER 13
WHERE YOUR TREASURE IS SO LIES YOUR HEART

Vision is a great attribute that has served St. Al's from its inception. The vision of our founding families helped the church to become an integral part of the neighborhood. Over the last 125 years we have seen many changes. Folks no longer come to worship here by foot, horse or wagon. The majority of our parishioners come from outside of our "parish boundaries." With all of the changes comes new and exciting challenges to serve the call of the gospel. In the following pages you will read about some pretty neat initiatives that have occurred or blossomed in the last 25 years. Our call for Social Outreach to meet the needs of our neighbors has grown and flourished through our Food & Clothing Center, Catherine's Care and the Creston Neighborhood Association. We offer a beautiful ministry through Funeral lunches that lovingly care for those grieving. Looking forward to the future as our forefathers have done led to the establishment of the Parish Foundation and Endowments. These two funds help to stabilize and guarantee the future of the Parish for the next generations. And finally with the completion this year of the Capital Campaign our campus is accessible to all and in wonderful physical shape. All of these have become a rich part of the legacy of St. Al's.

Miss Mary Wysocki and Harry & Dorthy Mika

ST. ALPHONSUS PARISH FOUNDATION

It takes a vision…… or in this case a Priest and Pastor with a vision! In 1984 during his "second tour of duty," Fr. Richard Quinn C.Ss.R. saw the need to "look ahead" to secure the future of financial challenges the parish might face. He began the process along with Rick Zambon, a parishioner who was also an attorney and Robert Bennett the Parish Business Administrator. Together they established the Parish Foundation under the guidelines of the Redemptorist Foundation that had been established in his home parish of Our Lady of Perpetual Help in Kansas City Missouri. The Foundation is set up to cover the capital needs of the Parish as well as assisting with the education of future Redemptorist priests. Other "founding members" and important contributors were Harry Mika who did all of the investing and growing of the account for many years as well as Tom Deschaine. And many other fine and dedicated volunteers have helped to direct, shape and grow this fund to what it is today.

When asked about why he felt compelled to establish this for our Parish his reply was "I liked the Parish so much that I wanted to insure that it would continue to be a vibrant and financially sound Parish." Fr. Quinn had the honor of introducing it to the Parish at his last weekend of the second assignment. He was also "blessed" to come back a third time and see that the tiny seed that he planted in 1984 had grown to over one million in less than ten years and continues to grow and contribute to the vitality of the Parish today. We owe a huge debt of gratitude to our three time Pastor and friend Fr. Richard Quinn. Your vision has secured the future to our next 125 years!

Rick Zambon, one of the founding members of the foundation, with Beth Zambon, Fr. Tom Donaldson and Judge Dennis Lieber

HER FUNERAL LUNCHES MAKE A DIFFERENCE

"After more than 35 years of preparing luncheons for funerals, Ginny Moroski was looking forward to handing her spatula over to another.

'I had a girl ready to take my place, but she ended up moving to Allegan,' she says.

Ginny Moroski, funeral lunches, September 2008

'Then two or three months ago, there was another possibility, but she retired and moved up to the U.P.'"

"She may be disappointed, but hardly angry, because she views what she does as a gift to others.

This year marks the 37th year that Moroski, 76, has been working the ovens, coolers, and 10-burner gas stove in the kitchen here at 224 Carrier Street N.E.

When she began cooking in 1971, Richard Nixon was president, 'All in the Family' was debuting on TV and Intel was introducing something called the microprocessor.

But the basic foodstuffs offered in the wake of funeral Masses here hasn't changed much since then—meats and cheeses, a variety of rolls and bread, salads and desserts. If the funeral is for someone of Polish descent, you can almost always count on kielbasa.

It takes a village. No less than a dozen women in the parish serve as monthly chairwomen, and they direct a cadre of volunteers numbering more than 180. "

"Though Moroski waves off the role she plays, Mitzi Zeilbeck, 84, lauds her as a colleague who does 'all the organization and planning of menus. It's a tremendous job, and she does it willingly.'

Funeral lunch ladies

Moroski is more apt to herald the efforts of all those who surround her in the effort.

'All I have to do is call 'em and ask, 'What's on your calendar for tomorrow? She says. 'And I know I can count on 'em.'"

"Moroski arrived around 9 A.M. with the funeral slated for 11 and the luncheon set to begin shortly after noon. She and others will stay until as late as 3 P.M. to clean up. It's a six-hour day of service for folks with whom she will have little contact."

"There's a sense of peace and warmth in this kitchen, women moving in little circles to uncover salads, cut cakes into squares, make sure the tables are just so.

It's the way Ginny Moroski has directed them for nearly 40 years, and so you're hardly surprised when, on your way out, Mitzi Zeilbeck touches your arm and says in a voice quaking with age, 'Want some fruit salad? I made extra.'"

Excerpts from: The Grand Rapids Press,
25 Sep 2008, Written by: Tom Rademacher

CATHERINE'S HEALTH CENTER

Discussion about creating a clinic to serve northeast Grand Rapids neighborhoods had been ongoing from at least 1993 in light of the limited medical resources available to the large population of low-income, under-insured people in the neighborhoods. St. Alphonsus Parish leaders including Fr. Jack Dowd C.Ss.R., Sr. Roberta Heffron O.P., Fr. Dan Lowery S.Ss.R. and Helen Lehman were part of the visionaries that helped to bring "Catherine's" to its inception. Both the Redemptorist order and the Grand Rapids Dominicans were some of the initial financial donors.

Catherine's Care Center was established in 1996 in the basement of St. Alphonsus Church. The clinic was started due to the closure by the Kent County Health Departments of the well-child clinic that had been located in the Creston neighborhood. Neighborhood organizers and the community felt it was critically important to have health services for children located within walking distance. Catherine's started as a nurse-run clinic offering immunizations, health education and free screenings primarily for children but it became apparent that the families of the children they were serving also had unmet medical needs. In 2000 a volunteer doctor joined the nurse and began offering free medical services two day per week.

Old Catherine's Care

Over the years in response to the growing number of uninsured and under insured in our community they have continued to expand services and to recruit volunteers and paid staff. In 2009 with too many turn-aways and very limited space

New Catherine's Care

they launched the "Opening Doors Campaign" and raised over $1.2 million. This allowed them to convert a vacated wing of our former St. Alphonsus Elementary School to a larger clinic in order to better serve the community. In 2011, under the name, Catherine's Health Center they moved into the re-purposed, LEED Gold Certified facility. They continue to offer general family practice care, completing more than 7,000 contacts annually while on track to expand their services to serve the working poor.

FOOD AND CLOTHING PANTRY

Following the charisms of the Redemptorist Fathers and the Dominican Sisters, our Parish began an outreach ministry led by Sr. Susan Ridley O.P. She along with Virginia "Ginny" Moroski opened what would be our first site of the food & clothing pantry at the corner of Lafayette and College. From it's humble beginnings over 40 years ago they have seen many changes in the neighborhood and the clients they serve. When the Dominican sisters moved out of the property at 205 Carrier it freed up space to expand the ever growing needs of the Pantry. By now the Parish was serving hundreds of cli-

Sr. Roberta Hefferon

ents a month. Through many generous benefactors and outstanding volunteers, Sr. Roberta Hefferon grew this tiny outreach into the vital ministry it is today. In 2012 they distributed over 57,000 lbs of food and served 7,498 individuals with clothing and household

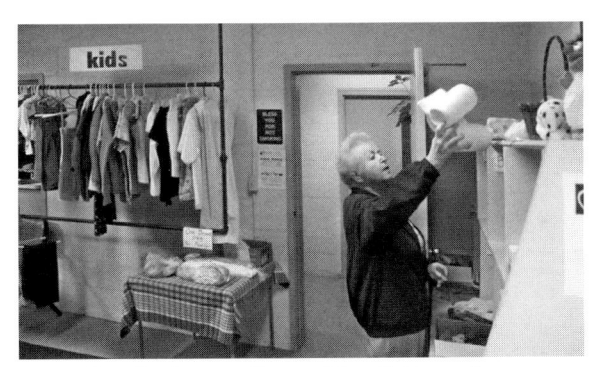

Sr. Roberta "stocking" the store

items. There was never a donation too large or small that this beautiful woman wouldn't chase after in a panel truck! She was a magnet for folks to embrace the ministry. Her legacy that she grew will now be moving into even larger facilities as they occupy their "newest home" in the Parish Center. They also provide "mobile food trucks" multiple times a month that supply fresh produce, dairy and bread to over 140 households. Twice a week St. Al's hosts free dinners in conjunction with God's Kitchen for those in need of an evening meal. They also sponsor "Meals to Go". Our current Social Concerns outreach also includes employment seminars to assist the unemployed in finding work as well as a free tax preparation service each year.

Sr. Roberta and Mike Hillary shopping

CRESTON NEIGHBORHOOD ASSOCIATION (CNA)

The Creston Neighborhood Association is located in the "old convent" of St. Alphonsus Parish and is closely tied with our parish. In the early 1980s, Charlie and Lucille Page saw a need to improve their slowly declining neighborhood. They invited their neighbors to their home for meetings, forming the Page St. Block Club. This grew into the CNA. Charlie serves as CNA's first president and Lucille served as its first secretary. Dee Kamsickas was a founding member of the CNA as well as a parishioner. Helen Lehman was one of the first directors serving from 1986-1995.

CAPITAL CAMPAIGN

"It takes courage to launch a capital campaign in the midst of one of the worse financial times in history" said Fr. Denis Ryan C.Ss.R. With faith we can do this!

We think those words spoke a courage that matched those of our founding fathers in 1888.

Taking down the Baldachin

Initial discussions had been ongoing to do some major work in the Church since 2002 when the first committee was formed. When plans were announced to consolidate our 120 year old Parish School the scope changed and widened. Not only were there items in the church that needed attention but now we had an quasi-empty school building that needed to be repurposed.

Committees were formed, input from every Parish group was prioritized and a plan took shape. John LaPorte, a generous parishioner and architect, worked tirelessly to flesh out the options after the needs had been gathered. In May of 2008 the plan was presented to the Parish during "Town Hall" meetings. And the courageous Parish embraced the plan!

Lead by Fr. Denis the core committee which included Bob Tobin, Tom Deschaine, Michelle Storey, Helen Lehman, Scott Schumaker, Sharon Kirkwood, Linda Parker, Bob Thiel and Dave Witt they worked diligently. Through the pledge phase over $1.9 million was committed to the plan. Improvements to the Church included tuck pointing, a new roof, a new heating system, repainting and refreshing. Marble was removed from the Baldachino (lowering it) so that the previously blocked stained glass windows could now be seen.

A fire suppression system was installed in the Rectory along with a new boiler (the old one had served the community well since 1919). A circle drive and landscaping in the front of the rectory allowed for easy drop off and pick up of parishioners.

In the Parish Center an elevator was installed and for the first time our building was accessible to all! Not to be missed a new boiler was also needed there. In addition the kitchen and dining area was freshly painted and updated. A new floor in the kitchen as well as barrier free bathrooms on the second floor were installed. The last to be completed projects are the Rectory offices to be moved to the Parish center allowing for barrier free access for all. The Food and Clothing Pantry will also move over to the Parish Center allowing for the extra space needed for their programs to grow and expand.

The campaign was completed in 2014 right on schedule and fully paid for through the generosity of the people.

ST. ALPHONSUS PARISH EDUCATION ENDOWMENT

It became clear in the 1980s that additional sources of funding were needed to keep the Parish School viable financially. Under the leadership of Phillip Haack (principal), the Home and School Association and the School Board the "Development Committee" was created. Their charge was to help cover the expenses of educating the children of St. Al's School that could not be covered under the regular parish budget. They researched grant opportunites and created a variety of fundraising options. They started the Fish Fry's, the golf outing, and the auction.

In 1998 the decision was made to formally begin an endowment fund to insure that the programs would continue into the next generations.

A 501©3 was established and through the generous seed money from the Grand Rapids Dominicans and the Development Fund, the Endowment was born. Multiple funding opportunities ensued from the "stained glass window" calendars and cards, to homecoming weekends, to raffles, the wall of fame, as well as the closing year of the school and the "dream team," and baccalaurette events.

Our charter and scope altered when the parish school merged with the schools of neighboring parishes to create All Saints Academy. We then expanded to include all educational endeavors in our parish.

Through the contributions of hundreds of donors and the efforts of scores of volunteers, the Endowment has grown to more than $950,000. These endowed funds provide the basis for grants and scholarships each year, supplying support for faith formation programs and tuition assistance for parish families enrolled at All Saints Academy. We also have been involved in capital improvements to our educational facilities, the youth programs and much more. It is a vital component in the finances of our parish, providing a permanent and sustainable source of funding for a variety of important needs that advance Catholic education and Faith Formation at St. Al's!

John and Jan Inghram, Auction

Rich McAuliffe, Steve Fryc, Don Nugent

Commands and Tobins, Pre-auction Party

Laura Stawasz, Colleen Tobin, and Linda Parker, Auction Night

Pat Byrne, Jim Kilbourne, and Doc Vincent

Tom and Arlene Hummel

CHAPTER 14
THE HISTORY OF OUR ORGANIZATIONS

The rich tradition of St. Al's has always been grounded in the wonderful people. The legacy that has been built for 125 years is one grounded in service and support.

Dick Nawrocki and Dan Fortier

We are highlighting a few that we have details on but this list is very long. Many groups that did many wonderful things were never written down and thus lost. See how many of these may jog your memory. And maybe you can add to the list!

CO-REDEMPTORIST

Just what is a Co-Redemptorist? It is people, who lend a hand in helping to educate young men who are discerning and journeying to the Priesthood. Over the years we believe that there have been hundreds of students from St. Al's who have gone off to Esophus, Edgerton and Glenview......to just name a few to discern the call.

Donna Krenselewski and Lucille Page

135

Mechele Duba and Diane Koepke

And the people of St. Al's have been there to support them with their prayers and their financial support. Do you remember the card parties in the '40s, the '50s and the '60s? Folks would pay to come and play cards with the proceeds going towards the support of the seminarians. We also have former grade school students tell of selling "Worlds Finest" chocolate bars that had the calories removed by Fr. Oelrich... could this be true? All of their proceeds from the candy sale went to help educate young seminarians. So maybe it wasn't so much the "Page Street" influence as much as it was those calorie free chocolate bars!

ST. GERARD'S GUILD

This group was inspired by St. Gerard Majella, the Redemptorist patron saint of mothers. St. Gerard's heavenly vocation is as a special protector and intercessor for women trying to conceive, for those wishing to have a healthy pregnancy or at the time of delivery. In short for all mothers of every kind and in every situation. The St. Gerard guild was active in the '40s, the '50s and '60s. These ladies would come together, sew and gather together layettes of clothing for those ladies in the parish expecting a new birth.

St. Gerard's Dance article, Vi Adomatis

There has been a renewal of the St. Gerard's Guild only now they are called the St. Gerard's Sew and Sews. This group of parishioners get together once a week and make prayer quilts, mittens, walker bags, clothing protectors and a variety of other items. These are distributed to those in need through the Parish Food & Clothing Pantry, the Michigan Veteran's Facility and through

125TH CELEBRATION COMMITTEE

In 2013 a group came together to begin to plan and oversee this historic event for our Parish by **"Embracing Our Tradition, Our Faith and Our Future."** The fruits of their labors were many. From the opening event on September 28, 2013 till the closing weekend of events, July 31 thru August 3, 2014, this group has lead the way. The "be kind" program with their "Acts of Kindness" tokens spread the message far and wide. Parish dinners with speakers nourished both our bodies and souls. We won't soon forget the spirited and spirit filled mission delivered for three days in February with Redemptorist missionaries Fr. Tony Judge C.Ss.R. and Fr. Maurice Nutt C.Ss.R. Spirits were energized with Steve Angrisano in song and praise in April of 2014. The Parish owes a debt of gratitude to all who planned, worked and attended to make this **QUASQUICENTENNIAL YEAR** memorable! God's blessings on the **NEXT 125!**

125TH STEERING COMMITTEE

Ken Fortier • Cindy Hodges • Carole Nugent
Joe Nawrocki • Dayna Bearss • Marla Marsala
Andrea Brandt • Fr. Patrick Grile • Paul Command

those traveling on mission trips to be distributed to those in need.

St. Gerard's Sew and Sews

JUNIOR CATHOLIC DAUGHTERS

This organization was really a Catholic version of the girl scouts. School aged girls from the Parish would meet once a week in an age appropriate group to work on projects. It was a youth program for girls 6-18 that was founded on the principals of faith working through love.

They would earn badges for their sashes by doing works of charity, learning crafts and doing projects. They had green uniforms and volunteer leaders that were often moms of one of the girls in the group.

Junior Catholic Daughters, 1963

Girl Scout Troop

HOLY NAME SOCIETY

Joe Nawrocki and Ken Fortier

Organized February 12, 1899 with 25 men from St. Alphonsus Parish. This was the first organized group in our Parish. They existed primarily for the spiritual betterment of it's members. They took an active part in the building up of the Parish including the building of our current Church. They were active in campaigns to raise money for the Church. They were also involved with the youth of the Parish and were the early advocates for the forming of youth groups. They would receive Holy Communion together as a group at least once a month.

CATHOLIC BOYS CLUB

Organized in 1903 as an offshoot of the Holy Name Society. This was an opportunity to "consider more closely the welfare of the young men of the Parish, and try to keep them out of public pool rooms" (quote from the Golden Jubilee book of 1949). They also promoted adding playgrounds and places of amusement for children.

LADIES OF THE HOLY FAMILY

Who doesn't remember this wonderful group of ladies who worked tirelessly to host May breakfasts and May crownings. They were also instrumental in providing new "make things nicer" in our Parish. For years (decades actually) they made vestments, altar cloths and

Mrs. Regina Patin and Mrs. Mary Schwartz

chalices when they were needed. We have heard that they made vestments for the Priests, not unlike the ones made by the St. Gerards Sew and Sews for our 125th anniversary. When there was a Priests ordination or a Jubilee to be celebrated, this hardworking team hosted many lovely and elaborate dinners to honor the priest. We owe so much to these ladies who taught us how to love through service.

Sacred Heart League...   *Organized in 1893*
The Altar Society...   *Organized in 1893*
Legion of Perpetual Help
Legion of Mary
Ushers Society
St. Vincent DePaul Society... *Organized in 1914*
Liguori Players
Boy Scouts
Parents Auxiliary Scout Club
Renew Groups
Ladies of the Holy Name
Junior Holy Name Society
Young Ladies Sodality
Married Ladies Sodality
Super Buddies
Angel Groups
PALS
His Helping Hands

Bearss Family at a parish picnic

Fr. Andy Thompson, Sirach Kurban and Quentin Florido

Louie Hillary, in the kitchen at the festival

CHAPTER 15
THE FOUNDING FAMILIES

One of the really beautiful things about St. Al's is that once you are part of the Parish family you will always carry a piece of the community with you. That is evident by the numerous families that are now into the 5th, 6th and 7th generation still attending the Parish. While we really don't believe that we have scratched the surface of identifying who all of these "founders" are, we are pleased that during this jubilee year we have been able to gather this wonderful information on some of these families.

FOUNDING FAMILIES

CALLAGHAN FAMILY

This history comes to us from Helen Foley and she has some clear history to share. She has aunts, uncles and her father that were all part of the founding of St. Alphonsus. Her grandfather, William Callaghan was a founding member of the Parish. Her uncle John Collins and her aunt Dora Callaghan were in the 2nd graduating class from St. Al's school in 1890. Her grandparents William and

Jack McGarry, May 1, 1927

Margaret (Anderson) Callaghan were married in the "new Church" which was the upstairs auditorium in the original School.

Bueche and Geske families

BUECHE FAMILY

Louis (Bueche) Geske is our historian on this family. Louise's great grandfather and great grandmother Henry and Caroline Bueche joined the "new" Parish of St. Alphonsus when it was established. They had 6 sons and 1 daughter. In 1900 Louise's grand parents were married in St. Al's. Louise's parents were also married at St. Al's in 1924. In 1947 Louise and her husband Don (deceased) were also married here. In 1975 Louise and Don's oldest son and daughter in law tied the knot…… and yes if you guessed at St. Al's you'd have guessed it correctly. The generations continue with the wedding of Louise's granddaughter in 2003, Stephanie (Geske) to Jake Weaver. Quite the lineage! All 4 generations of the Henry and Caroline lineage were baptized at St. Al's. The Bueche family has also contributed two priests to the Redemptorist order, Fr. Chuck Bueche (Louise's brother) and Fr. Bill Bueche (Louise's nephew). Fr. Bill is the offspring of Mary and Bill Bueche (Louise's brother).

Taylor and Saganski families

TAYLOR FAMILY

Phyllis (Taylor) Saganski filled us in on their connection to the beginning of the Parish. She believes that her great grandmother, Mabel Weeks attended St. Alphonsus School in the beginning years. Her father, Jim Taylor graduated from the School in 1925. She also believes that there was a Taylor descendent attending the School from 1889 until 1987 when her last child graduated from the school (four generations). She believes that they are related to the Grile family through the Parnell/Tallmadge township Byrne connection!

MCKAY FAMILY

Pat Rockwell is our family historian on this one. This family reads as a patchwork quilt of this Parish...... McCarthys, McKays, Bueches and Hummels and a large cast of offspring!

Charles Bueche (Pat's grandfather) was an offspring of Henry & Caroline Bueche. He married Agnes in 1900 at St. Alphonsus. From that came Lillian Bueche (Pat's mother) who then married Doug McKay on October 26, 1926. We loved hearing about the intertwining of the Bueche and McKay Families. And there are dozens of "offspring" who have attended St. Al's School and Parish.

Knight and McKay families

KNIGHT FAMILY

Our information on this family comes from Doris & Samuel Knight. Doris who is very involved with the geneology dept at the GR Public library believes that her husbands family roots trace back to the beginning years of the Parish. His grandfather married Mary McGinn on May 26, 1887 (marriage was not at St. Al's) but as soon as the new Parish formed, they joined. They lived on Hopson Street in the 1900s and walked to St. Al's for Church as they did not have a car. He was in the tile and asbestine business and she believes that he laid the floor that is under the main altar today. Samuel Knight was born in 1941.

RILEY FAMILY

Barb (Riley) Smith has a wonderful connection to the beginning of the Parish. Her great-grandfather was in the first rolls of the Parish. As was her grandfather and her mom and Dad (William and Dorothy Riley). Barb is the 4th generation to call St. Alphonsus her home.

O'NEAL/MAKSYMOWSKI FAMILY

The historian in this family is Mary Maksymowski. Her grandparents were Cornelius & Ellen (McManus) O'Neal. The attended the first mass for the new Parish of St. Alphonsus when it was held at

St. Johns Orphanage which was unfinished at the time. Mary's parents were Evelyn O'Neal and Al Simon. Mary has had five generations of her family go through St. Al's school. Her Uncle Jim graduated from there in 1903 and his graduation picture hangs in our "Wall of Fame!"

Edwards and Hefferan families

EDWARDS/HEFFERAN FAMILY

We got some great history from Mary Jane (Hefferan) Krajewski about how the Hefferan families traces back to the early days of our Parish in the late 1800s. She reports that her grandparents, Edward Edwards and Mary (Cummings) Edwards were founders of our Parish. All of their children attended the school. Her "great uncle," Bob Edwards actually was responsible for the artistic finials and columns on the ceiling of our Church as it was being built from 1906-1909.

He was from Holy Redeemer Parish in Detroit, MI, which was also a Redemptorist Parish. The architect and many of the craftsman that built Holy Redeemer were also involved in the building of St. Alphonsus. Mary Jane also said that her grandfather, Edward was part of the team that built the Rectory. And of course many members of the Hefferan family have been involved through the years giving service to our Parish. Mary Jane as our Parish Secretary, Larry Hef-

Madeline (McGarry) Lydell, 1925 First Holy Communion

feran in our music ministry and of course Sr. Roberta who for many years was the Director of St. Johns Home and then Director of Social Concerns here on our campus.

LARDIE/LYDELL FAMILY

Madelyn Lydell gave us some great info on her family. Her roots trace back to the early founders also. Her grandfather Lewis Lardie was the 1st burial from the "new Church" in 1909. Her aunts were the 1st double wedding from the present Church also on June 8, 1915. Blanche Lardie married John McGary and Florence Lardie to Cornelius Honton.

The angels on the ceiling of St. Alphonsus Church

ST. ALPHONSUS FIRSTS

Aug, 1888   St. Alphonsus Parish created

Aug 23, 1888   Redemptorists arrive; Fr Provincial Loewekamp & Fr Theodore Lamy

Sept 1, 1888   Redemptorists settle at 41 King Ct; Fr Lamy (superior), Fr Terrence Clark (assistant), Bro John Philpot

Sept 2, 1888   First Mass; Celebrant: Fr Theodore Lamy; 8 & 10:30; Location: The new orphan asylum building

Sept 2, 1888   First Baptism: Bernard Edgar Roche

Sept 9, 1888   First Sunday Catechism; 104 children

Sept 10, 1888   First Recorded Parish Death: Mary Stafford

Sept 15, 1888   Ground broken for St. Alphonsus School To serve initially as church, school, & priest's dwelling

Sept 25, 1888   First Recorded Marriage: James Tierney & Elizabeth Bird

ST. ALPHONSUS FIRSTS CONT.

Sept 27, 1888	First stone of St. Alphonsus Church laid on St Alphonsus de Liguori's birthday
Sept 30, 1888	First High Mass
Oct 14, 1888	School document placed in cornerstone & blessed
Oct 18, 1888	School cornerstone laid; 110 x 45 feet
Jan 6, 1889	Dedication of the new temporary church (Feast of the Epiphany)
May, 1889	Dominicans arrive to assume responsibility for St John's Orphan Asylum
Sept 2, 1889	St. Alphonsus School opens; 4 Dominican sisters in charge; 180 students

ST. ALPHONSUS FIRSTS CONT.

June 2, 1890	Closing Exercises held at Redmond's Opera House; First St Alphonsus School Graduate: Laetitia Traverse
Feb 12, 1899	First Holy Name Society in Grand Rapids organized; Pastor: Fr Patrick Henry Barrett; Meeting held at Shanahan Hall on Plainfield
1903	Catholic Boys Club formed, Affiliated with the Holy Name Society
Feb 17, 1906	Bids taken for church construction
June 6, 1906	St. Alphonsus Church cornerstone laid by Bishop Richter
	First church building erected since the diocese was formed

Lardie & Lambrix Family

Dec 22, 1909	Consecration of the new St. Alphonsus Church
June 1913	Old pastoral residence moved & made to face the same way as the church

ST. ALPHONSUS FIRSTS CONT.

Aug 26, 1913	Groundbreaking for the new school
1914	Silver Jubilee Celebration of St. Alphonsus Parish
Feb 19, 1914	Homecoming night to cap the Silver Jubilee

FLORENCE ANNA LARDIE (1887-1966)
CORNELIUS A. HONTON (1886-1958)
DOUBLE WEDDING. JUNE. 8, 1915 AT ST
ALPHONSES. WITH SISTER.
BLANCHE LULA LARDIE (1886-1979)
JOHN JOSEPH MC GARRY (1878-1969)

A Double Wedding on June 8, 1915

June 24, 1925	St. Theresa shrine blessed & dedicated
Mar 22, 1928	St. Alphonsus School fire
Feb 1929	Holy Name Society Minstrel Show
1929	Babe Ruth visits St. John's Home
Apr 21, 1931	New carpet for Santuary given by: Married Ladies Sodality, Young Ladies Sodality, Ladies of the Holy Name
Apr 29, 1935	Play performed in the school auditorium by the Liguori Players
Sept 19, 1937	First Service Squad; about 25 girls, assisted with 1st & 2nd grades
Sept 7, 1938	First school uniforms worn by 7th & 8th grade girls
1938	First Fall Festival held

ST. ALPHONSUS FIRSTS CONT.

Nov 6, 1938	St. Alphonsus 50th Jubilee
Dec 24, 1941	First Midnight Mass held in the convent, in the Dominican's little chapel *Also in the church, the first Midnight Mass in 15 years
Jan 30, 1942	Second Youth Party for students 15–18 years old
May 1942	Mother of Perpetual Help – Adopt-a-Yank; Many Holy Name Society members were in the armed services
May 1944	Collection for a new plaque for boys in the service, placed at the Shrine of Our Lady of Perpetual Help
Nov 1945	Catholic High School; St. Alphonsus Parish assessment: $80,000
Mar 1945	Fire in the school basement; Societies meeting place destroyed
1946	Parish divisions; Holy Name Society membership reduced from 611 to 446
1946	Parishioners asked to turn in War Bonds for a new convent
1946	The Baldachin was installed
Apr 1947	Holy Name Society Minstrel Shows restarted after the war
1950s	St. Gerard Guild; made of married & expecting women of the parish
Apr 23, 1955	Only school in Grand Rapids to sponsor two softball teams, 7th & 8th grades
June 8, 1956	First CARA Club meeting (Catholic/Christian Athletic Recreation Association)

ST. ALPHONSUS FIRSTS CONT.

June 14, 1956	Charles Page elected president of the CARA Club
May 5, 1957	Dedication of the new organ
Mar 16, 1964	Demolition of the old school building begins
Nov 29, 1964	(Sunday) New Liturgy of the Mass – altar facing the people; Also, commentator & reader by Laity; More English
1964	Laying cornerstone for new school, by Fr. Thomas Landers, CSsR
Lent 1964	First Friday confessions for students stopped
Oct 16, 1965	First English High Mass held at 9:30; Choir director quit when Fr. Langton insisted on vernacular mass by the choir, saying it wouldn't last
1965	Religious Education taught by Confraternity of Christian Doctrine
	Youth Club – held monthly dances, bought all the shrubbery on the grounds
Nov 7, 1967	Concerned Citizens of the 2nd Ward; Addressed integration on a local level
June 1, 1978	Ordination of Fr. Bill Bueche, Fr. Tom Santa & Fr. Gary Ziuritas C.Ss.R.
	First mass said together on June 3, 1978 at home parish.
May 20, 1979	Opening mass after the major renovation
Sept 1980	Pre-School program begins at St. Alphonsus School
Late 1980s	Dominican Sisters move to Shangraw house. Convent building becomes housing for Seniors.

ST. ALPHONSUS FIRSTS CONT.

1984	Parish Foundation Begins
1998	Parish Endowment Started
June 2008	Final Class of St. Alphonsus School graduates from our campus
Sept 2008	All Saints Academy opens

CHAPTER 16
OUR CURRENT ORGANIZATIONS

Here is a snapshot of what thousands of hours of volunteer efforts looks like! Along with many who were not available to have their photo's taken, this is a look at what "ministry" is today at St. Alphonsus. It is at the heart of living the gospel.

125th Anniversary Committee

Adult Education

Altar Servers

Arts and Environment

153

Capital Campaign Committee

Choir

Daily Lectors

Endowment Board

Eucharistic Ministers

Eucharistic Ministers

Faith Formation Catechists

Finance Council

Fish Fry

Food & Clothing Store

Food Trucks

Funeral Luncheons

155

Gardening Angels

Hand Bells

Church Cleaners a.k.a. Hell Gang

His Hands Ministry

Knights of Columbus

Lectors

156

PALS

Parish Council

Parish Store

RCIA Catechists

Right to Life

Sacristans

157

Sew and Sews

Sunday Catechists

Ushers

Dear Parishioners:

It is an old saying that figures speak for themselves. The Financial Report which we present to the people of St. Alphonsus Parish confirms this saying.

The year 1957 may certainly be considered one of the banner years of the Parish. With the loyal cooperation of the parishioners we were able to build an addition to the School - remodel the old School - install a new Organ, and take care of necessary repairs.

The Parish is now faced with a considerable debt; $50,000.00 on the Sisters' Convent and $245,000.00 on the School. During the current year we shall have to pay about $14,000.00 interest and $34,000.00 on the principal.

With the continuation of the plan proposed last year, namely, that every wage-earner contribute at least $3.00 in the Sunday Envelope, our obligation can be met. This is a plan now followed in many other parishes where they also have 25 cents seat-money and Grade School tuition.

All the parishes are also paying $116.00 per student in Catholic Central High School.

Anyone considering these facts and figures conscientiously, will realize his or her obligation to the Parish.

May God bless and prosper each and every one and may our Mother of Perpetual Help prompt all to continue their generous sacrifices for their holy Faith.

John J. Britz, C.Ss.R.

JOHN J. BRITZ, C.Ss.R.
Pastor

CHAPTER 17
OUR BEAUTIFUL STAINED GLASS WINDOWS

In 1919, St. Al's Pastor Mathias Meyer, CSSR, placed an order for stained glass windows for the church. The original order included eight nave windows, twenty-one sanctuary and transept windows, and one "rear" window. Later, ten smaller additional windows were ordered. The smaller windows included three in the baptistery, two in the sanctuary, two in the vestibule, two transoms in transept, and one in the stairwell.

1. ST. DOMINIC RECEIVING THE ROSARY

Our windows were designed and produced by the studios of F.X. Zettler, of Munich, Germany. Together, these 30 major windows and ten smaller ones throughout the church make up an area of nearly 3,000 square feet. The stained glass windows were installed in 1920, replacing the clear glass windows that were in place since 1909.

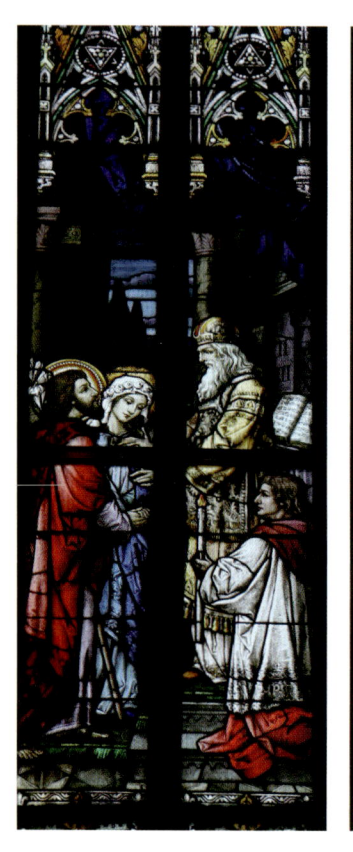

2. THE PRESENTATION OF MARY IN THE TEMPLE
3. THE VISITATION
4. THE ASSUMPTION

5. THE ANNUNCIATION
6. JOACHIM, ANN AND CHILD MARY
7. OUR LADY OF LOURDES

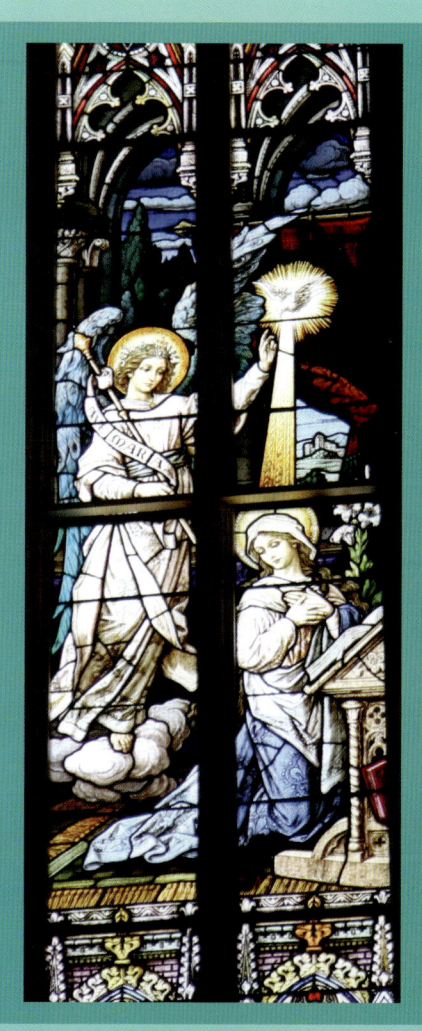

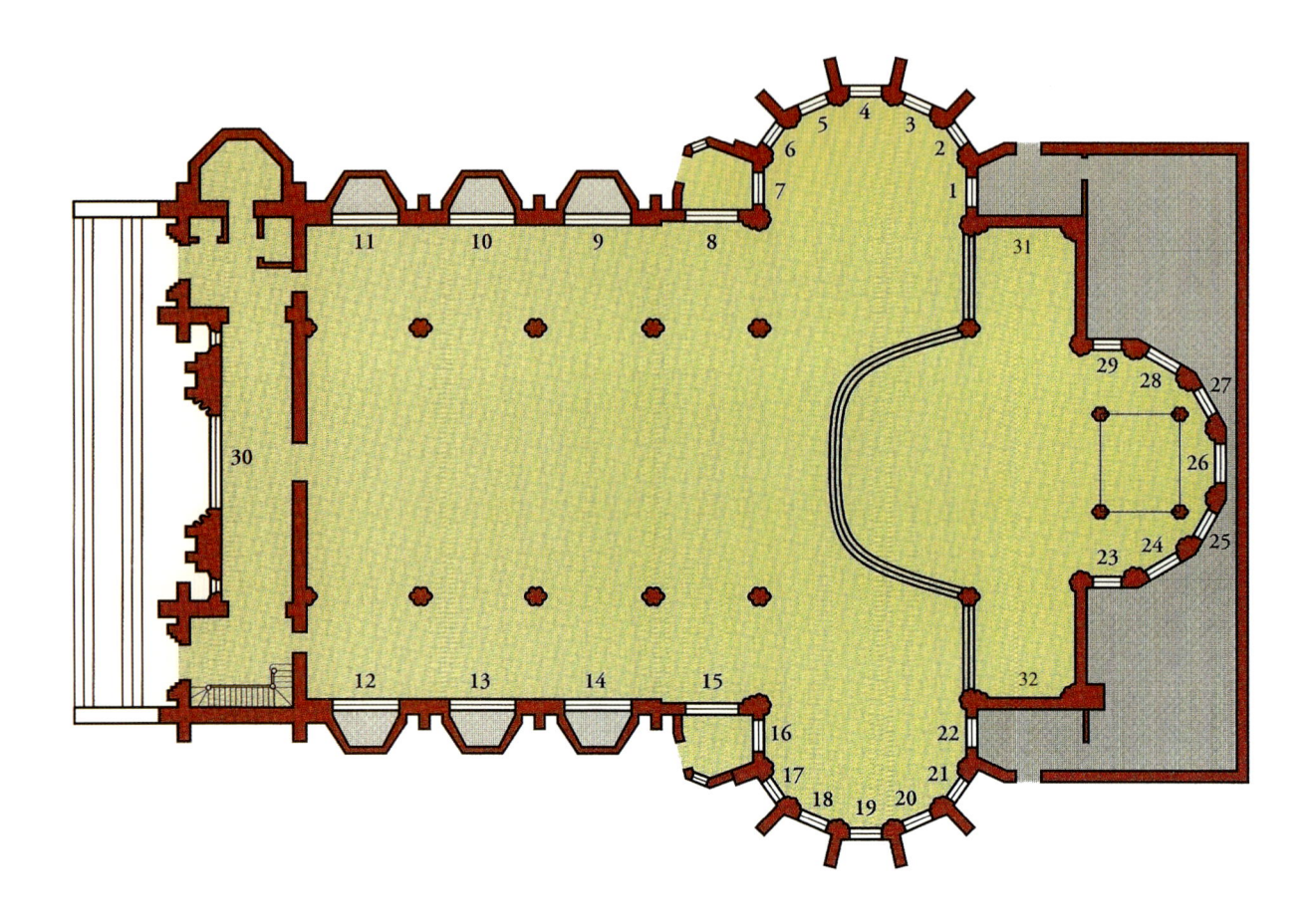

Stained glass is really not "stained". It's glass that's colored by adding different chemicals to glass in its molten state. Metallic oxides make the color: copper for ruby, manganese for purple, iron for green, etc. Flat sheets of glass of different colors are then cut into whatever shapes are needed for the design of the window. Strips of lead, the softest and heaviest common metal, hold the pieces together. It also resists the attacks of air, water, and pollution.

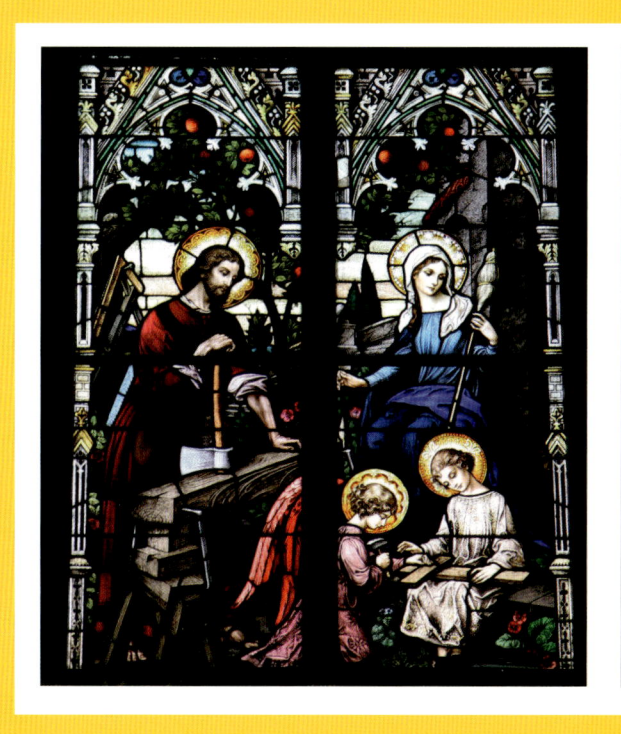

8. HOLY FAMILY IN ST. JOSEPH'S CARPENTER SHOP
9. SACRED HEART AND ST. MARGARET MARY ALOCOQUE
10. HOUSE OF PHARISEE, WOMAN ANOINTS FEET OF JESUS
11. GARDEN OF GETHSEMANI

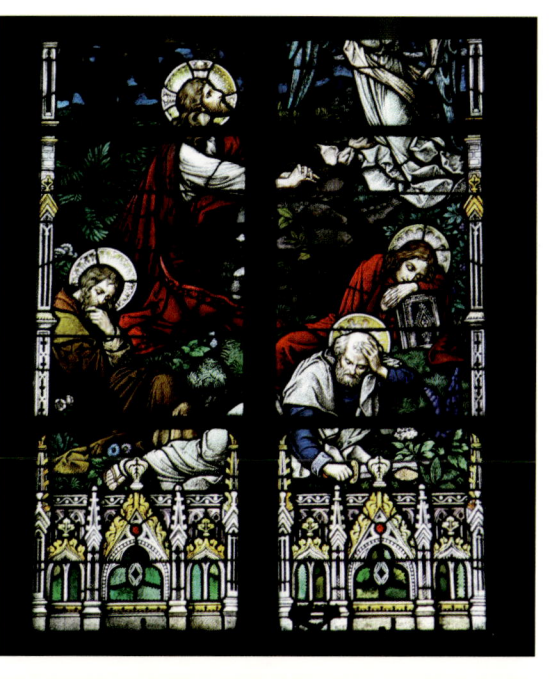

12. PETER RECEIVES THE KEYS TO THE KINGDOM
13. DEATH OF ST. JOSEPH
14. JESUS AND THE CHILDREN
15. REDEMPTORIST SAINTS: ALPHONSUS, CLEMENT AND GERARD

166

16. MARRIAGE FEAST OF CANA
17. PRESENTATION OF JESUS IN THE TEMPLE

Details in the windows, such as faces, folds in clothes, and words of text, are painted on the glass with enamel made from ground glass and rust powder mixed with glue. This mixture is then fired in a kiln to bond the enamel to the glass before it's leaded.

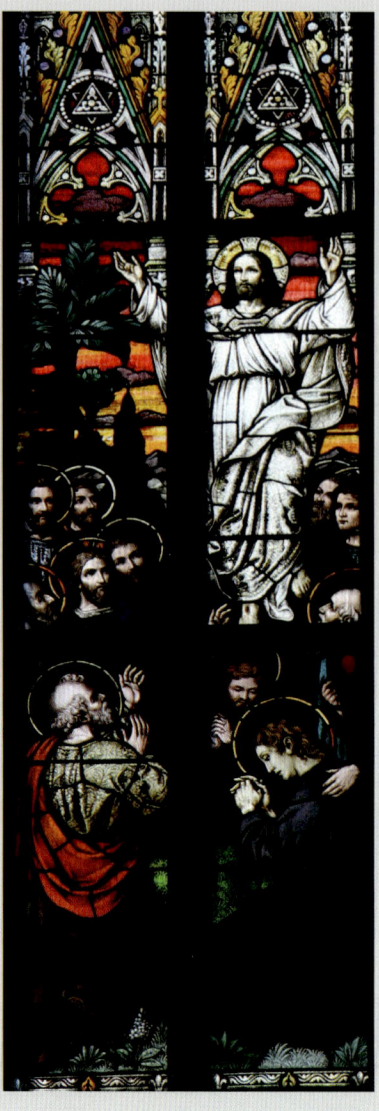

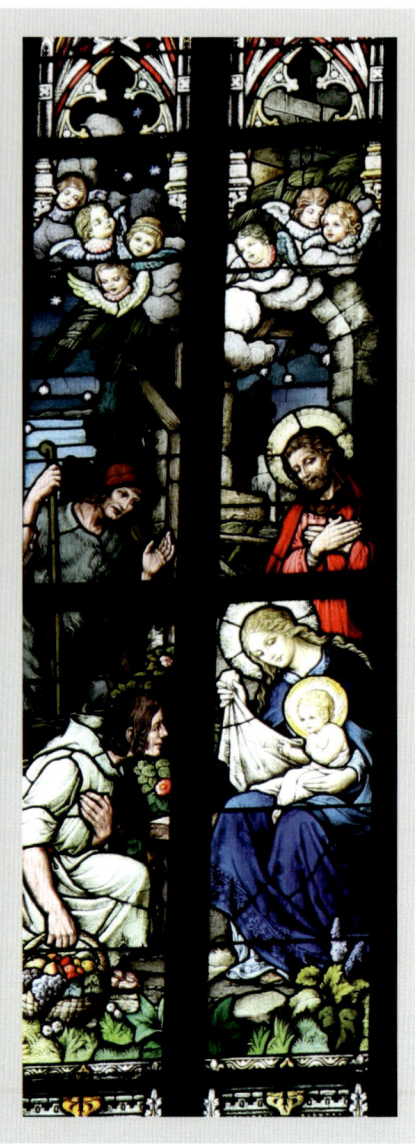

18. VISIT OF MAGI
19. ASCENSION
20. ADORATION OF THE SHEPHERDS

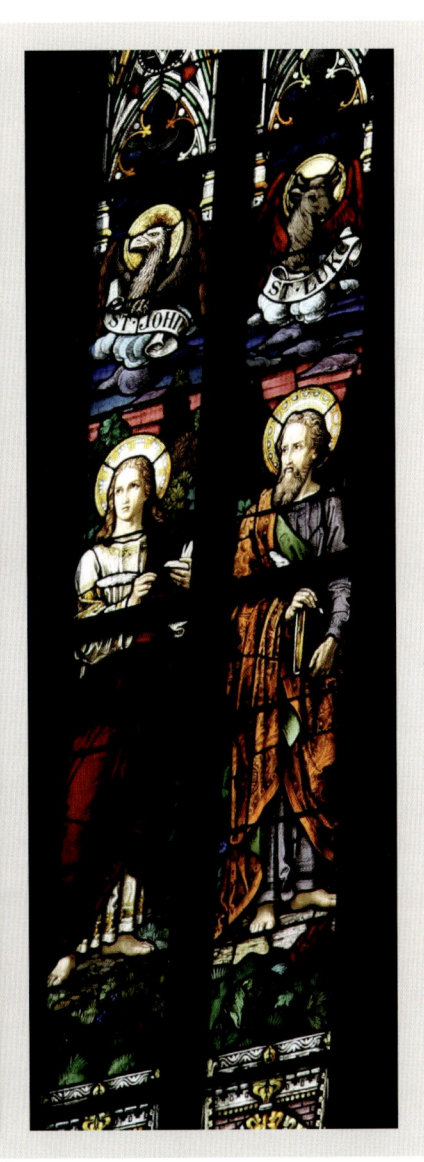

21. FLIGHT TO EGYPT
22. LOST IN THE TEMPLE
23. JOHN AND LUKE

169

24. DISCIPLES AT EMMAUS
25. MELCHISEDECH

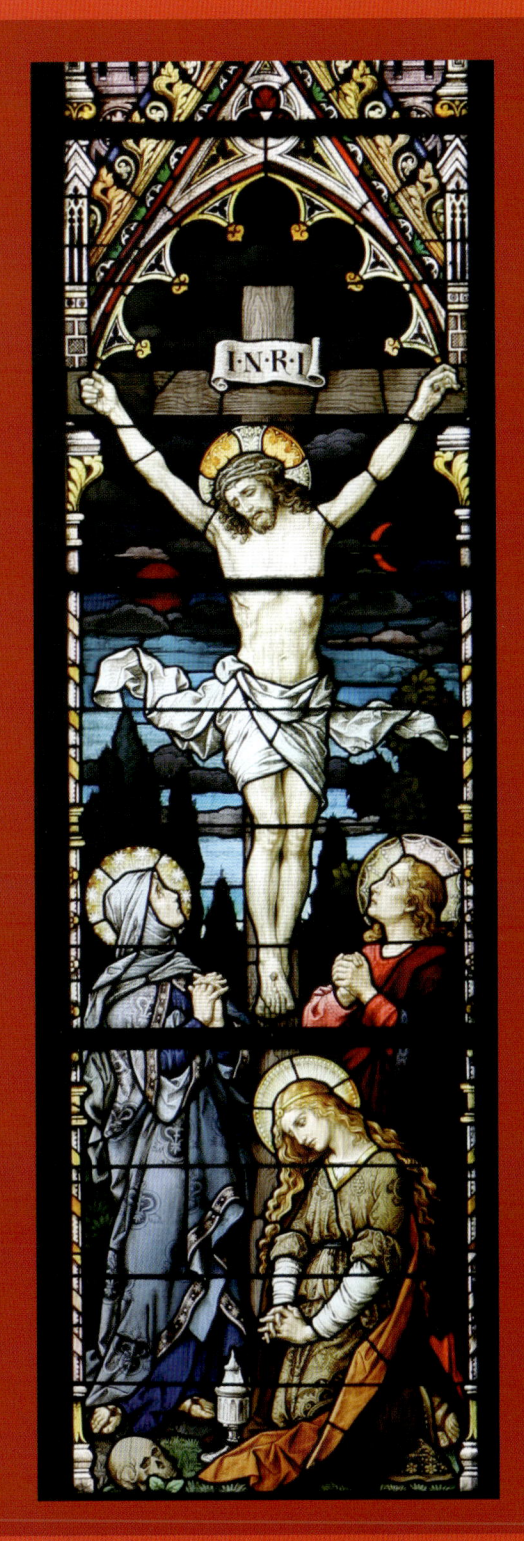

26. CRUCIFIXION
27. ABRAHAM AND SACRIFICE OF ISAAC

171

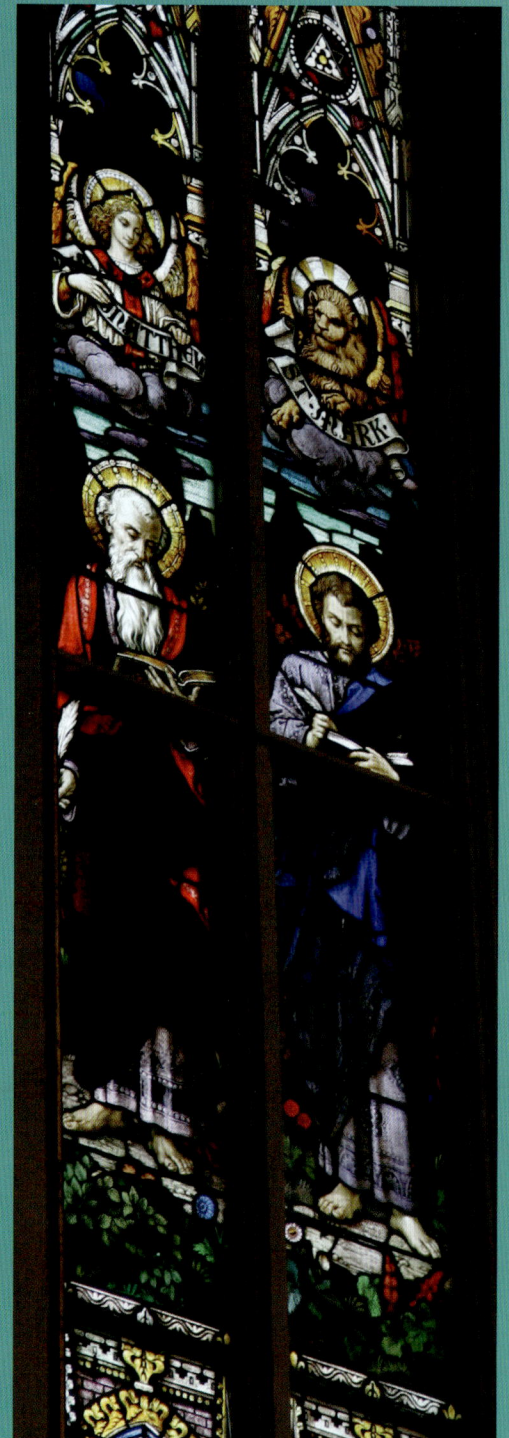

28. THE LAST SUPPER
29. EVANGELISTS: MATTHEW AND MARK

Stained glass windows do wonderful things with light. Unlike a painting or a mosaic, which reflect the light, stained glass lets light pass through the artwork. The light is colored, refracted, and spread throughout each piece of glass. Stained glass changes with the light, reflecting not only the weather, but also the mood and feeling of the day.

30. ST. CECILIA

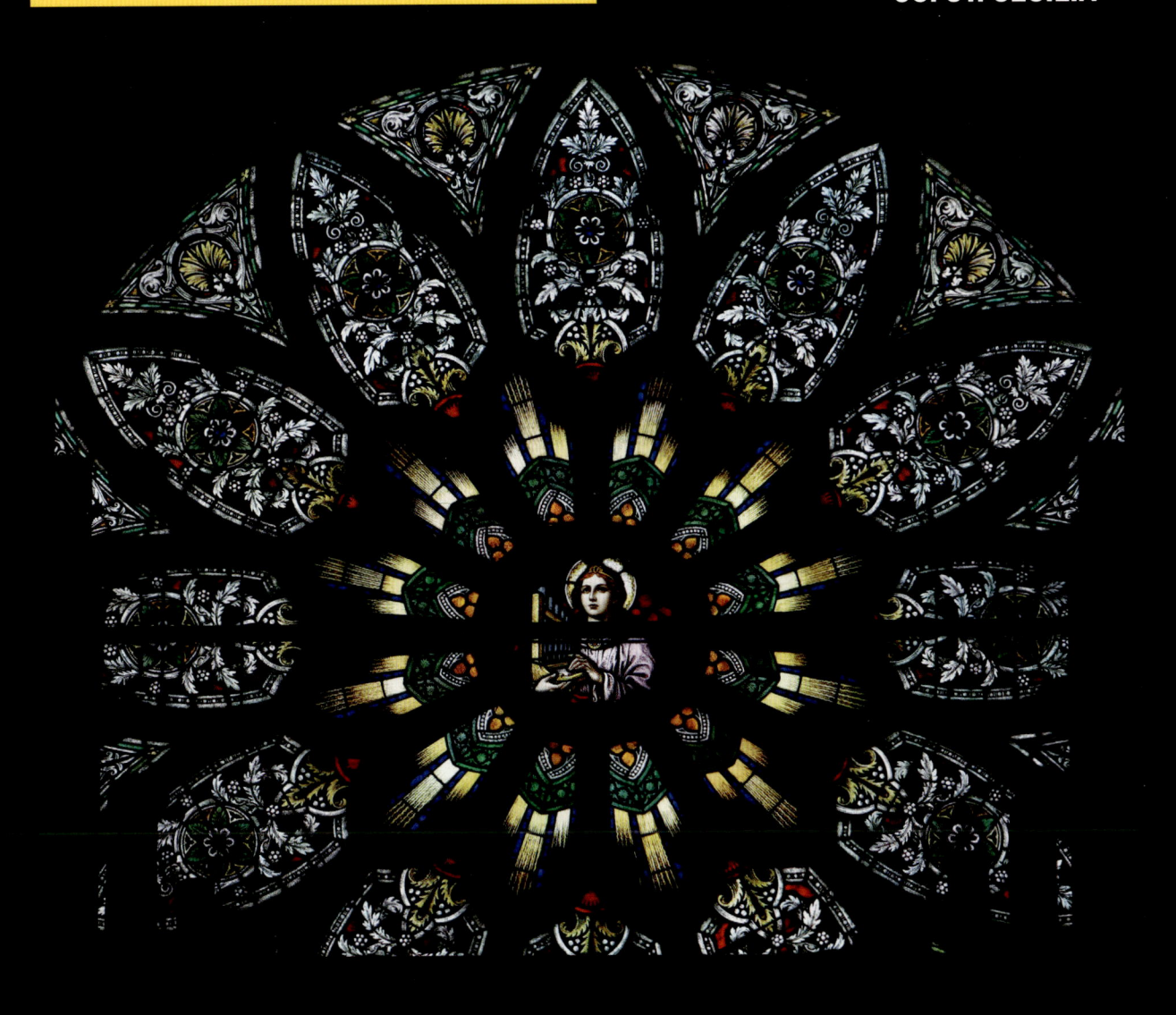

31. MARY SANCTUARY WINDOW   32. JESUS SANCTUARY WINDOW

125TH CLOSING MASS | AUGUST 3, 2014

125TH CLOSING MASS | AUGUST 3, 2014

CHAPTER 18
CONGRATULATIONS LETTERS AND PAPER PROCLAMATIONS

ST. ALPHONSUS PARISH PRAYER
For Celebration of our 125th Anniversary

St. Alphonsus, you are the patron of our parish faith community and our spiritual Father. Through your passionate love for our Lord Jesus and your intimate devotion to Mary, His mother, please pray that they bless this 125th year of our existence as a parish with many special graces.

May we always be grateful for the dear souls whose faith and tradition have blessed our parish these many years.

May the Spirit send down the fire of His justice and love into our hearts and inspire us to be people eager to respond to the Gospel message.

May that abundant love of God always be the gift we celebrate and the grace we seek to share with everyone who comes in touch with us.

We especially ask, St. Alphonsus, in your name and under your guidance that our Lord Jesus Christ and Mary, our Mother of Perpetual Help, lead us day by day to deepen our faith in God's will and purpose for our parish.

In gratitude we pray, Amen.

His Holiness Francis
cordially imparts the requested
Apostolic Blessing on
Rev. Patrick Grile C.SS.R. Pastor
and the People of the Redemptorist Parish
of St. Alphonsus
on the occasion of 125th Anniversary year of its Foundation
and through the intercession of the Virgin Mary
invokes an abundance of divine graces
Saint Alphonsus Parish, Grand Rapids, Michigan, USA
1 August 2014

Ex Aedibus Vaticanis die, 11 - X - 2014

Archiepiscopus Eleemosynarius Summi Pontificis

DIOCESE OF GRAND RAPIDS
Office of the Bishop

May 16, 2014

Reverend Patrick Grile
St. Alphonsus Church
224 Carrier St., NE
Grand Rapids, MI 49505

Dear Father Grile,

On behalf of the clergy, religious, and lay faithful of our diocese, I wish to extend to you, your Redemptorist brothers and parishioners, my heartfelt congratulations as you celebrate the 125th anniversary of the establishment of St. Alphonsus Church.

Many decades have passed since Bishop Richter, the first bishop of Grand Rapids, invited the Redemptorists to staff a newly created parish on the northeast side of Grand Rapids. Under the leadership of the Redemptorists, the parish has thrived as a vibrant Catholic community. The parish's fervent commitment to the spiritual, educational, and outreach needs of its surrounding neighborhoods has touched many lives over these many years. The fruit of such a fervent witness is the number of vocations to the priesthood and religious life that have sprung forth from the parish.

May the parish continue to be a beacon on the hill so that generations to come may know the joy of the gospel message and the embrace of a welcoming community of faith. God bless you on this historic milestone!

Sincerely yours in the Lord,

+David J. Walkowiak
Most Reverend David J. Walkowiak
Bishop of Grand Rapids

CONGREGATIO SS. REDEMPTORIS *Superior Generalis*

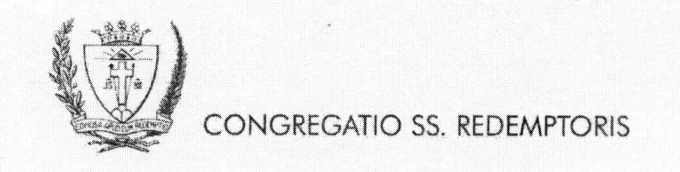

Roma, April 21, 2014
Protocol No. 4500 081/2014

Dear Confreres, Associates and Friends of the Parish of St. Alphonsus,

It give me great joy to greet you as you celebrate 125 years as a community of disciples of the Risen Jesus in Grand Rapids!

This time of celebration provides you with an opportunity to look back in gratitude for the wonderful ways in which the Lord has been present in the life of your community for more than a century. For 125 years, generations of people have walked through your doors – families, friends, neighbors. They came for many different reasons – to worship together, to pray together, to celebrate family occasions such as weddings and baptism as well as to mourn the passing of loved ones. Each of them, I am sure, found a place of welcome, a place where in good times and bad, they have felt the presence of the Lord and the support and friendship of the community. For this, you can say: "Let us Rejoice and Be glad!"

I am also told that over the years the young people of your community have been generous in responding to the Lord's call to service in his Church as priests and religious. In particular, as Redemptorists we have benefitted from this generosity. Twenty-two of my confreres trace their vocation back to your community. For this, as a Congregation, we can say: "Rejoice and Be Glad!

But your celebration is also a time to pause and take stock. It is a time to look at the present and the challenges the Lord sets before you as his disciples. We live in an increasingly complex and changing world where many of us are challenged in living out our faith – a faith that asks us to bear witness to the truth of God's presence and love in our broken world; to share that love with others, especially to those who feel abandoned and rejected, to the poor and the suffering. Oftentimes this is not easy. It is demanding. It is tiring. Sometimes it means carrying the cross. This is the cost of discipleship. But the rewards are great.

While this celebration is an opportunity for you to once again embrace your tradition and your faith which has sustained so many of your forebears, it also an opportunity to ensure that this tradition and this faith will continue as a precious gift that you will hand on to the generations that will come after you. What has held true for you in the past will hold true for you in the future: "Times change, but our faith endures!"

C.P. 2458 - 00100 ROMA - ITALIA   Via Merulana, 31 - 00185 ROMA - ITALIA

CONGREGATIO SS. REDEMPTORIS

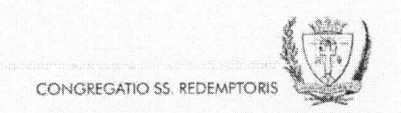

Friends, as you celebrate this wonderful occasion, may it remind you once again that you are called and sent by Jesus Christ to live gratefully the life God has given you and to proclaim the good news of Jesus Christ, the good news that promises God's "plentiful redemption to all." In a spirit of faith, service and community, may you continue to bring people closer together and to God, and in doing so build on what has been handed on to you by the generations that have preceded you and whom we remember in our thoughts and prayers.

With Every Good Wish and Blessing,

In the Most Holy Redeemer,

Michael Brehl, C.Ss.R

Fr. Michael Brehl, C.Ss.R
Superior General

Dominican Sisters
Grand Rapids, Michigan

May 16, 2014

Parishioners of St. Alphonsus Church
C/o Father Patrick J. Grile, CSsR
224 Carrier Street NE
Grand Rapids, MI 49505

Congratulations to St. Alphonsus Parish Community!

Dear Father Grile and Members of the St. Alphonsus Faith Community,

Best wishes and blessings to you, the parishioners of St. Alphonsus Church, and our Redemptorist brothers during the celebration of your Quasquicentennial Year. Your theme "125 years of Embracing our Tradition, our Faith, our Future" captures the faithful dedication of your parish through decades of growth, and the years of fine leadership of the Redemptorists. You all have great cause to celebrate how your witness and service has touched, nurtured, sustained and encouraged spiritual growth among parishioners, in the Grand Rapids Diocese, in your Northeast neighborhood and around the West Michigan area.

What a blessing that we Dominican Sisters, as your neighbors at St. John's Home for orphaned children and teachers at the parish school, could collaborate with such holy pioneer people of the parish from its very beginning. St. Al's school served to educate the mind, body and spirit of each individual child who walked through the classroom doors. This legacy should bring much pride to all parishioners who sacrificed and actively participated in building such a wonderful family of believers.

It has been an honor to have served with, prayed with, and celebrated many milestones with such a faith-filled Catholic community. Your welcoming spirit, your generous outreach over the years are shining examples of seeing needs and responding to people out of sincere respect and love – all in imitation of Jesus' own life and ministry.

We celebrate with joy the good work God has begun through you and will continue to foster in the many years of ministry ahead. With St. Alphonsus we pray: "Give me a burning faith, a joyful hope and a holy love for Jesus Christ."

In Saints Dominic and Catherine,

Maureen Geary, OP
Prioress

Sponsorships
Dominican Chapel Marywood
Dominican Center Marywood
Spiritual Formation Program
Retreats/Conferences/Seminars/Workshops
Associate Program
Prayer and Listening Line

Ministries
Education/Health Care/Chaplaincy
Parish and Diocesan Ministry
Partners in Parenting
WORD Project
-ESL Program
-HASD Program
Maternidad, Chimbote, Peru
San Pedro Sula Ministry, Honduras

Advocacy
Advocacy for Justice
Care of the Earth
Culture of Peace
Global Partnership
Ending Homelessness

Emboldened by faith, serving with joy

2025 Fulton St East
Grand Rapids, MI
49503-3895

T (616) 459.2910
F (616) 454.6105
www.grdominicans.org

SAINT ALPHONSUS CHURCH
REDEMPTORIST
224 CARRIER STREET, N.E., GRAND RAPIDS, MICHIGAN 49505
PHONE (616) 451-3043

May 14, 2014

Brothers and Sisters of St. Alphonsus,

God is good all the time! And we have certainly witnessed the goodness of our God during our 125th Anniversary Year!

Let us be so grateful for the blessings that God has given us as a parish community. I think of all the baptisms, weddings, funerals, and sacramental celebrations that have taken place over these 125 years and I am humbled and thrilled at the same time. Who could count the moments of joy that have occurred as new life was born into families? And of the celebrations of marriage which began new relationships and families? And the tears of sorrow that were shed as lives ended but were surround by the hope and belief of Resurrection? And the thousands of souls healed by forgiveness and nourished at the Table of the Lord? And the many who were comforted with the sacrament of the sick and received peace of mind? And the sons and daughters of our parish who were ordained as priests and those who professed their vows as religious?

God has poured out countless blessings upon us over these past 125 years!

Let us embrace our traditions that have guided us so well.

Let us embrace our faith that has been the foundation of our giving and loving.

Let us embrace the future with confidence and hope.

May St. Alphonsus, our patron, and Mary, Our Mother of Perpetual Help, keep us faithful to our commitment of being Christ for others in the years to come!

In the Redeemer,

Fr. Patrick J. Grile, C.Ss.R.
Pastor of St. Alphonsus

THE REDEMPTORISTS — DENVER PROVINCE

1230 S. Parker Road
Denver, Colorado 80231
PHONE 303-370-0035

www.redemptorists-denver.org
information@redemptorists-denver.org
FAX 303-370-0036

OFFICE OF THE PROVINCIAL

August 2014

Dear People of St. Alphonsus Parish,

Congratulations on your 125th year as a parish!

When the present church was built in 1906 a writer in the *Michigan Catholic* said in part: "The church, which stands on an eminence overlooking the valley of Coldbrook, with its two tall spires pointing heavenward, will stand as a monument for all time to the magnificent faith, the undying hope, and the exquisite and heroic charity that been exemplified in such marked degree in the small, yet great congregation of St. Alphonsus." High words of praise, indeed!

As you celebrate 125 years as a parish I think the sentiments expressed by the newspaper writer in 1906 remain true. St. Alphonsus people have been known through the years for their "magnificent faith," their "undying hope," and their "exquisite and heroic charity."

An anniversary is a time to remember the past, with gratitude. The parish has experienced periods of stability and periods of change. You have had your ups and downs. Through all the good days and not-so-good days the Lord has been there leading and guiding and you have followed with magnificent faith.

An anniversary is a time to give thanks for what we have today and to celebrate. It is especially good to celebrate those who went before us in faith and the ones who keep the torch of faith alive today. We thank those who with exquisite and heroic charity have served the parish and the community. I, for one, am grateful for the example of the Redemptorists who served at St. Alphonsus and for the excellent schooling I received at St. Al's School from the Marywood Dominicans.

An anniversary is a time to look forward with "undying hope." We build on the past and in the case of St. Alphonsus Parish that is a good and strong foundation. So we can look to the future with undying hope.

St. Alphonsus, pray for us. Mary, Mother of Perpetual Help, continue to pray that we will be faithful, hopeful, and loving people.

In the Redeemer,

Fr. Harry A. Grile, C.Ss.R.
Provincial – Redemptorists – Denver Province

P.S. Yes, my brother Pat and I are two of the many Redemptorist vocations from Page Street.

CHAPTER 19
MEMORIES

This book is a wonderful journey into the history of the last 125 years. As we stated many times the stories and the book is about all of the many hearts that have made St. Al's home for all of us. We "surveyed" some folks to share with us what their fondest memories are. We invite you to add your memories to the last page. And please write them down so that the next generation continues to see the wonderful legacy that built this parish.

A moment that has always stuck with me is when I held the tiny hand of my first born child, Shannon and walked with her into kindergarten orientation. I was greeted by Mrs. Hesse who promptly looked at me and told me to "march right back out that door." Mrs. Hesse was a teacher at St. Al's when I went there and was actually the supervisor when I was a cheerleader. She just couldn't handle that a former student was standing in front of her—now a young mother! Dedicated teachers like Mrs. Hesse, Miss Wysocki, and Mr. Sieracki who made a difference in my life and then in my children's lives is what made it all worth it. I feel very proud and blessed to call St. Al's home. —*Mary (Hillary) Ketelaar*

Choir rehearsals with Joan Bueche, Bruce Doornbos, Liz Sarafis and then to be able to direct one of the finest music programs ever! The "folkies", the choir, recording studio, Gerry Davis, Adam Stone and Todd Evans. Concerts in our Church by David Haas, Mark Forrest and Grayson

Warren Brown. Cantatas from "It took a Miracle", "The Dark Hours" and "His Last Days". Who could forget Christmas Carols with Fr. Balser as Santa! Doesn't get much better than this. —*Michelle (Robach) Ogren*

In grade school, we went to daily morning Mass and because of the "fasting" rules at the time, we could not eat breakfast before Mass. We carried our "breakfast" to school…which was often a scrambled egg sandwich. We had time at the beginning of the day to eat, and then started with classes. Our 4th grade classroom was up at St. John's Home. Boy did we love it when the "Sister cook" was baking cookies for the residents as it just smelled wonderful. Often we were able to taste the goodies! Mary Waters Park was our noon hour playground. During the winter we could bring our ice skates to skate. Plus we had Sister Janet Mish who loved to play softball with us on the field over there! Our 2nd grade classroom was under the stairway going into the girls bathroom. Sister Norberta was our teacher and was always so patient with our "journey" to/from the cafeteria! —*MaryEllen Novakoski*

Bingo. One of the "rights of passage" as a St. Al's 8th grader. Miss "Y" would take our class down on Tuesdays right after lunch and we would set up the cafeteria and gym with tables and chairs for that weekly fundraiser. It earned us money for our 8th grade class trip to Cedar Point. I would also be able to work at bingo, selling pop and popcorn. Mr. DeMario and Mr. Murray would always tell me to "go ahead little Hummel, you can have another donut but don't tell anyone." They made the best popcorn!! The New Year's Eve parties, which were always a sellout. My dad, Tom Hummel, sold tickets every year for this event. I learned as a small child how to give directions to our house so that people could come and pick up their tickets. And Tom Barnes coaching girl's softball for years… he had such patience! —*Mary (Hummel) Deschaine*

I only came to St. Al's on Christmas Eve and only to put a check mark in the "good son-in-law" box with the Neering family. One year my wife Gretchen pointed me in the direction of the RCIA program. I was a lapsed Baptist and went just to satisfy my academic curiosity!!!! Before I knew it I took the express lane and was baptized, had First Communion and Confirmation all at the Easter Vigil. That progressed into assisting with the RCIA program for 10 years. I am a proud Christian and member of the St. Al's family. Thanks be to God and Gretchen! —**Doug Clarke DVM**

St. Alphonsus provided so many treasured memories from my childhood, from the family atmosphere to the special touches the teachers and administrators put into each day. From Mrs. Hesse that would hug and console me when I was separated from my mom, to Mrs. Neva who made spelling a great competition, to Mrs. Williams who inspired my passion for reading and writing, to Mrs. Cordes who brought music and choir into learning, to Mrs. Crampton who defended her students and championed their growth, and Miss "Y" who really prepared us for higher levels of learning. Mrs. Dawson and Mr. Haack were great listeners, helpers and gave great guidance to us all. I had a blast through every school assembly, arts and crafts bazaar, parish festival and the all school Masses. It was a great way to grow up: feeling Jesus' love here on earth and certainly at St. Al's! —**Amy (Parker) Fox**

We remember the lasting friendships we have made over the years. The Cara Club's New Year's Eve dances which started out as formal dances with tuxedo's and ball gowns. The Cara Club took care of all of the sports activities along with hosting many fundraisers that helped the Parish.
—**Tom & Arlene (McKay) Hummel**

I remember getting a call from the St. Al's rectory during the Advent season in 1978. The secretary asked if I could please bring my children and come to Church because they needed a picture of a child looking at the outdoor manger that was on the front lawn of the rectory. I bundled up my son Dan who was about four and walked over to Church to find Fr. Mike Hillary and a reporter from The Grand Rapids Press. There had been a robbery and the Blessed Virgin Mary and Baby Jesus were missing… stolen during the night. The reporter took the picture of poor, sad, Dan looking at the empty manger. In the article Fr. Mike said he was praying the thief would return the missing statues. The next morning Fr. Mike went out and there was Mary and Jesus right back where they belonged. We had a Christmas miracle right here at St. Al's! —**Mary Hormuth**

In the late 1970s when I was in 9th grade, my classmates and I returned to St. Al's to make our Confirmation. My Aunt Duce was my sponsor. As we were walking out of the school to process over to Church, she slipped on the ice, fell and broke her wrist. First, I remember never seeing such a disfigured arm! Then I thought, "Oh no, I don't have a sponsor. Now I can't make my Confirmation." I don't remember who took my aunt to the hospital. I barely remember the bishops "slap". But I do remember Sr. Vera Anne stepping up and saying "don't worry Eileen, I will stand in for your aunt." Thank you Sr. Vera Anne! —**Eileen (Eyk) Domagalski**

My fondest memories are that my husband Terry and I were married at St. Al's 47 years ago and it has been an important part of my life ever since. Our children went to school there and our oldest daughter, Kim taught there for 11 years. The Religious and the members of the community have always been so supportive and caring. I am proud to say I am a member of St. Alphonsus! —**Barb Farrey**

I enjoyed playing on Mary Waters field during recess and talking about *NSYNC with my girlfriends. We would share Beanie Babies and make secret handshakes and the world was our playground. How many of us made forever friends on the St. Al's playground? —**Audrey Genautis**

Things I recall from my school days at St. Al's in the 1960s: great lessons from the Dominican Sisters, who were joined by an increasing number of lay teachers throughout this era. Sweaty football practices at Mary Waters Park. Safety duty, and hot chocolate afterward on wintry mornings. The May crownings and the pageantry. Redemptorists popping into the classroom-bringing tricks and treats. Lots of hours in the gym, with basketball practice in the afternoons, big crowds at the annual "Tournament of Champions" hosted by the CARA club, student assemblies in the daytime, special evening recitals and programs with parents in the audience. Fun, times, terrific people and great memories!
—**Bob Tobin**

I have soooo many wonderful memories about the students, parents and staff. One special one was the Christmas breakfasts that Mr. Haack and I would provide for the teachers and staff. What a banquet! And there was always fun and laughter. One year Fr. Jack Dowd, our newly assigned Pastor, attended to find our usual comic relief (Michelle Ogren, Linda Parker and Juli Lillis) showing up in pajamas with an always funny skit to perform. I am proud to have been a part of this community for 15 years. We all worked together and worked hard to make the school the best in Grand Rapids. I look back fondly at those times and think of them as our "Camelot years." —*Pat Dawson*

In 2nd grade Mrs. Jirous taught her students to always say a prayer when they heard a siren. She said that anyone who was in an ambulance needed it from us. So we would always stop what we were doing in class and pray for that person. It is a wonderful habit that remains with me today! —*Sarah Eyk*

All the boys in the 8th grade were in love with Sr. Marie Michael in 1967. She would play baseball with them at recess at Mary Waters Park. After lunch it would take a while for everyone to settle in and get down to our school work. If the boys were fidgety, Sr. Marie Michael would whip an eraser past their ears missing them by only mere inches. They were crazy about her because they all knew that she could hit them if she wanted! —*Mary (Eyk) Jeakle*

I was fortunate and blessed to grow up a member of St. Alphonsus. My best memories… Brother Matthew twirling a baton in front of the Church on his way to visit us on the playground. Sr. Emma's presence… And I mean her "presence". She needed nothing else. Her presence stopped everyone. Fr. Ernie Larson giving us a retreat in the 8th grade… so inspiring. Fr. Fagan's stories about his ministries on the Amazon river. I could go on forever…I just LOVE St. Al's. The Redemptorists, the Dominicans and all of the people. Goodness abounds from each and everyone. —*Theresa (Novakoski) Robinson*

My first experience with St. Al's was volunteering for Auction! I met many parishioners and learned a lot—who knew you could have that much fun volunteering! It was a great opportunity to see the wonderful St. Al's spirit at work behind the scenes. —*Dayna Bearss*

My memories of the great band concerts and potlucks of the '70s. Sr. Marie Rachel, Miss Wysocki, Mr. Mitri Zaniea and all the great teachers. The winter carnivals, field days at the end of the year and being a safety and an altar server. Home basketball games with the carpeted walls of the St. Al's gym! Also special was the Faculty/8th grade basketball games. —*Glenn Bearss*

I looked forward to preschool so I could play in the sandbox that was in the classroom! —*Layne Bearss*

I thought that it was cool that all of us students got to run down the hallways at dismissal on the last day the school was open. I still like seeing my tile that I made in 2nd grade on the large cross that hangs in the stairwell. —*Grant Bearss*

One year the students decided to compose and illustrate books that they could donate to DeVos Children's Hospital. We had all the students work on this project in their Angel groups—groups composed of students from each grade level. These books were laminated and then given to the Hospital in the hope that these books would provide some joy and entertainment to patients who were seriously ill. —*Mary Wysocki*

In the 1979/1980 school year I was in the very first pre-school class offered at St. Al's. In 2007/2008 my oldest daughter Monica was in the last pre-school class to be offered at our campus. It was an honor to open and close this program. —*Sarah (Parker) Hormuth*

YOUR MEMORIES